WOMEN'S INTERNATIONAL LEAGUE FOR PEACE AND FREEDOM

WOMEN'S INTERNATIONAL LEAGUE FOR PEACE AND FREEDOM

The Quest for Peace in South Australia

RUTH RUSSELL

Perspicuous Press

Published by Perspicuous Press in 2022.

ISBN 978-0-6451422-8-0 (paperback)

Copyright © 2022 by Ruth Russell

All rights reserved. No part of this book may be reproduced in any manner whatsoever without written permission except in the case of brief quotations embodied in critical articles and reviews.

First Printing, 2022

Contents

Foreword vii
Introduction xi

1. Women's International League for Peace and Freedom in Australia   1
2. WILPF Forms a South Australian Branch   28
3. First Nations Australians, the Settlement of South Australia, and WILPF's Campaigns to Seek Redress for Aboriginal Peoples   44
4. WILPF SA's Involvement in the Vietnam War, 1962-1972   63
5. WILPF SA Branch Peace Campaigns, 1980-2000   83
6. The Illegal US War on Iraq, 2003   102
7. United Nations Security Council Resolution 1325 on 'Women, Peace and Security'   116
8. SA WILPF, 2005-2014   124
9. WILPF Centenary Celebrations, 2015   137

About The Author   154

Foreword

History matters. It helps us to understand the world we live in. *Herstory matters*. It recognises the role that women play in influencing society, culture, politics, the economy, beliefs and goals. Women's stories need to be told, acknowledged and preserved, to be handed down to the next generations.

I am a proud member of the Women's International League for Peace and Freedom (WILPF). My pride stems from being a part of a significant international organisation which has an explicit *feminist* orientation in supporting women and building gender equality as intrinsic components of a *feminist peace*. I am honoured to write this foreword.

I haven't participated in much street activism because my main contribution is as a University Professor, researching and writing on peacebuilding, especially women's active participation in maintaining peace and security, during and after violent conflict. My peace activism involves teaching students ways to think creatively and to act constructively to minimise or prevent violent responses and instead, to enhance peace, justice and reconciliation.

I have supervised PhD students' theses on topics consistent with WILPF visions of a feminist peace, such as on: post-conflict transformation in Rwanda; women's NGOs in building peace in the Republic of Macedonia; Iraqi women's experiences of survival; transforming approaches to conflicts and disputes in Cambodia; motherhood discourses and equal opportunities; the war on terrorism; human rights; women's rights of Liberian and Afghan women in multicultural

Australia; women leaders in Local Government; and faith and women in Northern Ireland.

As I read this book, there are three significant conclusions to make. First, across Australia, WILPF covers a diverse range of peace issues. Second, WILPF members actively seek collaborations with like-minded groups. Third, there is a bold tenacity about WILPF members that motivates their ongoing work. Let me elaborate a little on each point.

First, peace is not merely the absence of war. For a positive peace to exist, a sustainable peace that is not so fragile that it breaks down with the slightest murmur of conflict, the root causes of injustices, inequalities and conflict must be addressed. WILPF members pay attention to anything and everything that might aid the progress toward realising peace and freedom. These concerns include overcoming patriarchy; achieving all forms of justice and equality; working for human rights of Australian Aborigines, prisoners, Pacific and Torres Strait Islander women, war victims, sufferers of domestic violence, and asylum-seekers and refugees; opposing nuclear arsenal and the dominant military mindset; demanding the disarmament of weapons; and suggesting curricula to enhance an education for peace. Peace is multifaceted, and WILPF works hard to build this.

Second, a peaceful world is collaborative and cooperative, yet differences of all types often work against productive engagement. In the stories in this book, there are many wonderful examples of WILPF members working harmoniously with other like-minded groups on mutual concerns. Where there are significant differences between individuals and groups, perhaps of religious beliefs, cultural nuances, or preferred strategies for invoking change, sensitivity to uniqueness and different personalities is needed. I love the phrase used in this book, that WILPF is willing to adopt 'friendly compromise,' but realise that for these women, this middle ground is never a conceding on the importance of feminist peace.

Third, what you might not pick up from reading these stories, but I can vouch for, is a persistent doggedness in working toward a sustainable peace, a determination not to give up, a constant badgering away, a refusal to take 'no' lightly, a steadfastness to continue, whatever the challenges. This personal drive impacts on local, state, national and international endeavours to build peace, in individual and collective endeavours. I remain sincerely impressed with this resolve to keep chipping away at obstacles that prevent human flourishing and the development of a sustainable peace.

Herstories - stories told by our sisters, daughters, aunts, nieces, mothers, grandmothers and women friends, influence the communal tale of how we come to be who we are. This book tells of a long history of South Australian women's activism for peace and freedom. The legacy of these women is enormous in helping to build a better world, one where human welfare is the priority.

But WILPF SA members are aging. There are a lot of grey headed women present around the table and on Zoom calls. More young, vibrant women are needed to assist this ongoing, lifetime peacebuilding process, and start creating their stories that will influence the next decades. Together, women of all ages can build a world where peace, justice, equality and reconciliation interconnect.

Professor Elisabeth Porter (Lis)
(Editor of this book by Ruth Russell)

Author of books on peace:

Porter, Elisabeth, *Women-of-faith Peacebuilders*, Imprint: Independently published, 2018.
Porter, Elisabeth, *Connecting Peace, Justice, & Reconciliation*, Boulder, COLO.: Lynne Rienner, 2015.
Elisabeth Porter & Anuradha Mundkur, *Peace and Security: Implications for Women* Brisbane, University of Queensland Press, 2012.
Bagshaw, Dale & Porter, Elisabeth eds, *Mediation in the Asia-Pacific Region: Transforming Conflict & Building Peace*, London: Routledge, 2009.
Porter, Elisabeth, *Peacebuilding: Women in International Perspective*, London and New York: Routledge, 2008, 2007.

Porter, Elisabeth & Offord, Baden, eds., *Activating Human Rights*, Oxford, New York & Berne: Peter Lang European Academic Publishers, European, 2006.

Dr Elena Spasovska, Dr Fatin Shabbar, Professor Lis Porter, WILPF seminar, 'Women and War: An International Women's Day Event,' 2021

Introduction

Ruth Russell (B.Ed, Dip T) was WILPF Australian National Coordinator for five years and WILPF SA Branch Coordinator for more than ten years, elected in 2012.

Let me tell you our story as peace activists, involved in all the major political issues of our time as members of *Women's International League for Peace and Freedom - SA Branch*. We proudly wear the badge designed by our foremothers with a peace dove and our name.

The *Women's International League for Peace and Freedom* (WILPF), initially called the *International Committee of Women for Permanent Peace* until 1919, was established at the Women's Peace Congress, convened by the *International Congress of Women* in The Hague, in 1915. Today, WILPF has member Sections in 39 countries and Consultative Status with the United Nations. What a proud history and what wonderful stories we tell of women's determination and activism to create a just and peaceful world.

International Congress of Women, The Hague,
28 April 2015

In 1999, WILPF International created a *Reaching Critical Will* project to lead the organisation's advocacy for disarmament and calling for an end to nuclear weapons. We are still waiting for sufficient countries to sign on to the ratification to make the end of nuclear weapons a reality. This project represents WILPF in many networks, such as the *International Campaign to Abolish Nuclear Weapons* (ICAN).

In 2017, ICAN was awarded the Nobel Peace prize for this initiative to rid the world of nuclear weapons. I was proud to chair a meeting in Adelaide with Gem Romuld, Director at ICAN Australia, who brought the Nobel Peace prize medal to show us at the WILPF seminar, *The Global Humanitarian Quest to Eliminate Nuclear Weapons: The Story So Far*. What an honour to be part of this movement to create a better world.

Gem Romuld, holding ICAN Nobel Prize medal with Ruth Russell, WILPF SA Coordinator, 2018

It takes a lot of organisation, knowledge, energy and time to get involved in trying to change the way our governments are responding to world events. Mary Heath, a well-known local activist and song writer expressed this so well with a song she wrote for protestors standing outside the Adelaide Convention Centre several years ago opposing a Defence Weapons Expo. Her lyrics went like this:

I would rather be swimming in a swimming pool
I would rather be lying back and keeping cool
I would rather be home in bed - but
They are selling weapons here, so I'm here instead.

While demonstrating by the stairs to the Convention Centre for this Defence Expo, I quietly said to a Japanese man as he stepped onto the escalator to register for this Expo – 'Remember Hiroshima'. About ten minutes later, the Manager of the Convention Centre came down to say someone had upset one of their delegates. I told her what I had said and that this was exactly the response we wanted – people to reflect on the use of weapons with all the destruction they wrought, so that we can work to rid the world of all armaments.

Hear our story and then come and join us.

1

Women's International League for Peace and Freedom in Australia

To understand the history of the Women's International League for Peace and Freedom (WILPF), South Australia (SA) branch, and all the wonderful work of the SA members, some background is needed.

Australian Federation

The movement to gain federation of all the new states into one nation was led by Alfred Deakin. Through his delegations with the British government, Deakin brought the six separate colonies together to form one nation. In 1901, the new nation, the 'Commonwealth of Australia' was born.

In 1902, the Commonwealth Parliament passed the uniform *Commonwealth Franchise Act* enabling white women, twenty-one years of age and older, to vote at federal elections. Interestingly, it also allowed for Aboriginal adult voters in all states except Queensland and Western

Australia to vote at federal elections, but few did so.[1] This right was soon removed under later legislation.

Federation brought a feeling of agency and self-reliance with the belief that Australians could mould their own destiny. At Deakin's insistence, Australia was to establish its own navy as Britain was too far away for swift action, if needed. Women who had formerly been relegated to wives, daughters and home-maker roles, now saw the potential to take an equal place beside men to build a great new future.

Deakin's values came from his friendship with the charismatic Reverend Charles Strong (1844-1942) who became his spiritual advisor. Strong had been charged with heresy by the Presbyterian Church in Collins Street, Melbourne, for supporting the opening of the Melbourne Public Library and Art Gallery on Sundays and treating women as equals to men.[2] Strong resigned from his position and took many liberal followers with him, including Deakin and Eleanor Moore. In 1885, Strong's followers established their own liberal church, naming it the *Australian Church* and built an imposing building with a huge pipe organ in Flinders Street, around the corner from Parliament.

Women associated with this progressive *Australian Church*, including Jessie Strong, the Reverend's wife, were determined to maximise their opportunity to create an inclusive and peaceful society.

The Vote

For Australian women, inclusion in full life as citizens required the vote. Without suffrage, women had a less significant role in public life, taking seriously their responsibility for managing their family, household and charity work. More women wanted to be involved in how their lives were affected by governments. They worked diligently in all states to achieve the right to vote. White female suffrage was granted over time.

1895   South Australia (second in the world after NZ)
1899   Western Australia
1902   New South Wales
1903   Tasmania
1905   Queensland
1908   Victoria

Aborigines and Torres Strait Islanders did not receive the vote for federal elections until 1962, and in all States in 1967.

Gaining the vote lifted the ambitions of many women who wished to act publicly for the good of their society. They were determined that women should take equal responsibility for the way their society behaves and is shaped. They wanted their views to be heard and acted on in parliament.

Increasing numbers of women were determined to participate more fully in the direction that their new nation, Australia, would take. They connected with suffragettes worldwide, believing that women should have an equal place in how societies are organised.

Most women were religious and took to heart the saying, 'Do unto others as you would have them do unto you.' They were determined that women should take equal responsibility for the way their society behaves and is shaped.

For the first time in history, women were educating themselves and organising into groups to improve the lives of those around them. They wanted to use their vote so their views could be heard and acted on in parliament.

Consequently, many women's groups developed to further their aims. WILPF was but one of them. The women knew they had first to educate themselves on each issue so they could develop an answer to the situations before them.

The next step was to speak out to broaden support for their views with the goal to influence both federal and state governments to enshrine laws that would promote peace, justice, equality and freedom (as their name implied).

Their first focus was on stopping young boys and men being drafted into war as they knew so well that violence never solves a problem and war is simply the ultimate version of violence.

These women inspire us with their tenacity and determination to not remain silent when issues of injustice, prejudice and 'power over' marginalised groups occurred. It is every citizen's right to live in a just and equal society. But this needs constant vigilance to ensure it happens. It is every citizen's right to speak truth to power.

These women spoke their truth to power as they wanted to live in a decent, fairer, peaceful world. War and discrimination are the furthest distance from that ideal.

Sisterhood of International Peace

Melbourne women suffragists who founded WILPF in Australia in 1915 sparked a women's peace movement that continues to this day.

In Australia, January 1915, Reverend Strong gave an address to the church titled *Women and War* in which he suggested:

> Women of Australia should form a league of peace...Think what a moral influence such a league would have...by exchange of literature, lectures and conferences, educating each other and educating the young! Women helped found Christianity. She was called now to aid in bringing the new patriotism, the new cosmopolitanism, with their new social conscience.[3]

On 25 March 1915, thirty women met at the *Australian Church* against a background of opposition to government legislation for compulsory military training for schoolboys and the involvement of Australia in a

European conflict. These women understood that the Constitution of the Commonwealth 1901, laid the foundation of the new nation, Australia, on social justice, universal education, democracy, freedom and the repudiation of war.

They were enfranchised and had seen Vida Goldstein stand for election to parliament. Most of these women peace activists were vigorous members of more than one international peace organisation. They were confident that as women they had an important role to play in working for peace through negotiation. Their firm belief was that all disputes are capable of resolution via arbitration *not* war. These activists named themselves the *Sisterhood of International Peace* – and their membership grew to around 210 members.

Sisterhood Committee - Mabel Drummond (left), Eleanor Moore (centre)

The Sisterhood's first task was to respond to the First World War which had commenced in July 1914. Their focus was on stopping young boys and men from being drafted into war. The Australian War Memorial suggests that 416,809 Australians enlisted. This was 38.7 percent of the 18-44-year-old male population, and that 61,522 Australians died (8,709 at Gallipoli).

There was already a tradition of women's internationalism through the suffragette movement, so the emergence of a peace specific internationalism in 1914-15 was a logical extension of a pre-existing tradition. Australian women had a proud history of using internationalism as a tactical political instrument for domestic gains.[4]

Early Australian WILPF Women

The invitation to be part of a women's international conference being held in The Hague, Netherlands, in 1915, was taken up by three Melbourne women, Eleanor Moore, Vida Goldstein and Cecilia Johns. They sailed immediately to get to the conference on time.

On 15 April 1915, while the three women were travelling by boat to The Hague in Europe, the Australian and New Zealand Army Corps (ANZAC) as part of a British Imperial Force, invaded Turkey. They landed at Gallipoli with appalling loss of life on both sides.

Ten days after the disastrous ANZAC Gallipoli landing on 25 April 1915, Moore, Goldstein and Johns joined 1,200 women from both warring and neutral nations in the Peace Palace in The Hague, Netherlands at the International Congress of Women.

The pertinent question was posed: *What would women do differently?* Congress participants came up with their *Principles of Permanent Peace* which had three main themes:

- Prevent war;
- Take away the guns (disarmament); and
- Create an international forum where countries could mediate to resolve conflict.

The women then disbursed and met the heads of European States and US President, Woodrow Wilson, to promote their *Principles for Permanent Peace*. President Woodrow Wilson's daughter, Eleanor, was an active member of WILPF USA. She influenced her father to adopt the women's *Principles* and to set up an International Committee to meet as soon as World War One ended.

WILPF was granted Consultative Status with the League of Nations (later renamed the United Nations in 1945 and based in New York USA). WILPF's office in Geneva today organises UN conferences around human rights.

On Eleanor Moore's return to Melbourne, the *Sisterhood* decided to affiliate with *Women's International League for Peace and Freedom* and officially became the *WILPF Australia Section*. Soon afterwards, the *Women's Peace Army formed* on 8 July 1915 with flamboyant Vida Goldstein as its driving force. Both women's groups had the same aim (to stop war) but different tactics on how to achieve it. WILPF women preferred to work through educating women while Vida adopted more provocative, public protests, driven by her committed pacifism.

When these women first met in Melbourne on 25 April 1915, Australia was already involved in World War One. At the same time as the women's peace conference in Europe, ANZAC troops had landed at Gallipoli. For Mrs Warren Kerr (Vice-President of the Sisterhood), it was a personal tragedy. Her son was one of the first of the 8,709 ANZAC soldiers killed in that battle. Her grief made her more determined to work for peace. She declared herself thankful that at least her son had died before he had time to kill another mother's son. She published at her own expense, the following plea urging young women to question war. She started with a quote from Winston Churchill:

> No operation in history is worthier of being pushed on with the utmost vigour, and an utter disregard for life, than at Gallipoli. I regarded it as a legitimate war gamble for a prize of inestimable value. [5]

Then Mrs Kerr (wife of the Bank of Melbourne Manager) writes:

I think it was then that the iron entered my soul and I finally decided what my life's work should be. Was it my loved one's life they gambled with? Was his one of the lives to be 'utterly disregarded'? How do I, his mother – how do all the mothers – live through it all? What a horrible injustice! What a degradation of motherhood! What a subjection of womanhood! Have you no hearts? Who can utterly disregard this?... Make it now your life's aim to help in the world-wide women's movement to abolish war. [6]

The anti-conscription contribution by women in the *Sisterhood of International Peace* was significant.

WOMEN'S INTERNATIONAL LEAGUE FOR PEACE AND FREEDOM

'The Blood Vote' flyer, 1916

Conscription
and Woman's Loyalty.

By ELEANOR M. MOORE.

I AM A WOMAN. I can only be loyal in a woman's way. I cannot give to the State what is not mine. Giving away other people's money is not generosity; it is theft. Voting away other people's liberty is not patriotism; it is persecution. Forcing other people to risk their lives for me is not courage; it is cowardice.

I AM A WOMAN. I was given a vote that I might impress my womanly feeling and point of view on public life. If I use that vote to strengthen men's faith in violence and revenge as against intelligence and moral force, my influence is worse than wasted.

I AM A WOMAN. I deny the right of any man or State to force me to produce life against my will. On the same principle, I recognise that I have no right to force any man to take life against his will.

I AM A WOMAN. Australia has given me the rights of citizenship. In return I must do my part to save Australia from becoming a prey to the militarism which has brought Europe to ruin. I see that, but for conscription, the present war would have been impossible. I must keep Australia free from that curse while yet there is time.

I AM A WOMAN. I have an obligation to the men at the Front, but I know I cannot relieve them by swelling the number of sufferers. I believe the glory of man is not in his brute strength and violence, but in his powers of intellect and spirit. For the relief of the agonised youth of all nations, our own included, I demand that he use these powers to bring the present war to an end.

I AM A WOMAN. I know that the idea that lasting peace can be gained by war is nonsense. I know that no war, however victorious, has ever produced lasting peace. I know that a just and honourable peace, such as the people of all belligerent nations are thirsting for and ready for, has a far greater chance of being permanent if arranged by negotiation than if brought about in any other way. I know that, however long the fight continues, in the end it MUST be settled by negotiation.

I AM A WOMAN. I know that everywhere and always, when men make war on men, the sufferings of such as myself are indescribably horrible. I know that as long as war continues such suffering cannot be prevented or mitigated. For this reason I will not sanction the war system by forcing any man to be a soldier.

I AM A WOMAN. For the honour of womanhood, for the glory of Australia, and for the encouragement of men to be true to the highest in them, I mean to record a vote of WANT OF CONFIDENCE IN WAR, and

Vote NO !!!

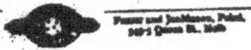

Authorised by T. J. Miller, Lees Street, Bentleigh.

Eleanor Moore's pamphlet, 'Conscription and Woman's Loyalty'

World War 1 Ends

Germany formally surrendered on 11 November 1918, and nations agreed to stop fighting while the terms of peace were negotiated.

In 1919, US President Woodrow Wilson chaired an international meeting in the Versailles Palace, France, to finalise the Treaty of Versailles which officially brought World War 1 to an end. He also called for a *League of Nations* to be established, offering mutual guarantees of political independence and territorial integrity to great and small nations alike.

It was agreed to establish this new international institution, based on WILPF women's *Principles for Permanent Peace*, in Geneva. Eleanor Moore was the Australian representative on the *International Committee* which met in the Hague Congress again after the war ended in 1919 where they formally named themselves the *Women's International League for Peace and Freedom (WILPF)*. On Eleanor's return to Australia, the *Sisterhood* became the Australian Section of WILPF in 1920, but we count as beginning from 28th April 1915 when the *Principles of Permanent Peace* were finalised.

Eleanor Moore travelled to Geneva to help establish a WILPF office there so that WILPF women could work closely with the new *League of Nations*. The Covenant of the League of Nations went into effect on 10 January 1920, formally instituting the League of Nations. By 1920, forty-eight countries had joined.[7]

Although establishing the League of Nations was largely the work of US President Wilson, America did not join the League. This was for several reasons – first, America had suffered civilian casualties in the war and second, many people in the USA wanted to keep America out of European affairs.

World Disarmament and WILPF Australia

During the first World War, every peace movement in Australia included disarmament in its program.[8] WILPF women in Melbourne felt they still had work to do – they wanted full disarmament, so set to work to achieve it. As mentioned, the *Principals of Permanent Peace* formulated at the International Women's Peace Congress in The Hague, became the founding document for the establishment of the League of Nations in Geneva.

WILPF World Disarmament Picnic, Melbourne, 1921

In 1931, WILPF women actively campaigned for the disarmament of all world weapons as proposed by the League of Nations after World War One, but sadly, not honoured.

Mabel Drummond (in the photo below, standing on the podium with a feather in her hat), was another long serving WILPF woman. This historic photo shows her addressing a huge crowd of men at a disarmament rally in Melbourne in 1924. For forty-four years Mabel also

WOMEN'S INTERNATIONAL LEAGUE FOR PEACE AND FREEDOM

worked with Reverend Charles Strong to publish and distribute widely their monthly *Peacewards* journal, a truly remarkable partnership, until his death in his nineties.

Disarmament Rally with WILPF Mabel Drummond, 1924

Mabel Drummond,
1933

In 1928, the *League of Nations Kellogg-Briand Pact* was formed. This was a *General Treaty for Renunciation of War*, as an instrument of national policy. Sixty out of sixty-eight nations, including the 'big powers', agreed to settle disputes by peaceful means.

For four years, WILPF women around the world organised petitions to support the *League of Nations' International Declaration for World Disarmament Conference* planned to be held in Geneva in 1932. Australian women planned to gather 100,000 signatures but finished by collecting 117,740 signatures across Australia. They had gone door knocking, talking to groups and to all and sundry, often carrying copies of their petition in their apron pockets, so they could collect as many signatures as possible.

Women from new WILPF branches in Hobart, Rockhampton and Newcastle also contributed to make this the biggest hand-collected petition ever put to the League of Nations.

Disarmament petitions with 117,740 signatures collected by hand

WILPF Victorian Executive with Eleanor Moore sitting with petitions

Eleanor Moore wrote in her memoir:

On November 30, 1931, at a memorable meeting in the Melbourne Town Hall, convened by the League of Nations Union and the World Disarmament Movement, a procession of members of the Women's International League for Peace and Freedom, presented bundles of signatures to the Prime Minister, in the presence of politicians, leading churchmen and other prominent citizens. The speeches made, recognised the magnitude and significance of their achievement. A similar accolade was given to WILPF women around the world when a total of twelve million signatures were presented to Geneva. Among these, Australia's contribution was the highest percentage per head of population in the world.[9]

The world leaders (all male politicians) could not agree to limit and reduce their armaments. The 1932 *Geneva Conference* failed to achieve what the people of the world had hoped for. Eleanor Moore writes

'No peace aspiration of our time had held out so bright a prospect of fulfilment; none led to such utter disappointment.'[10]

How history might have changed if the men who voted against disarmament at the League of Nations had supported the World Disarmament vote! Eleanor Moore writes in her account:

> The Russians summed up the situation well by saying the way to get disarmament was to disarm. But apparently when it came to the point, that step was a too great step from habit. Either the delegates or their governments behind them, lacked moral courage to do what they had all declared to be *the* only right thing to be done.[11]

Geneva, 12 million WILPF petitions stored in the League of Nations office

World War Two: 1939-1945

WILPF women restated their pacifist position. They protested about large increases in making armaments and profiting from that expenditure. They called on women to unite for peace, to ponder the waste and tragedy of war, and to insist that alternative and sane methods be used for settling disputes to save civilisation from disaster. As earlier WILPF women passed on, others joined and took on the peace issues of the day.

The United States detonated two nuclear weapons on the Japanese cities of Hiroshima and Nagasaki on 6 and 9 August, 1945. In Hiroshima, the explosion wiped out ninety percent of the city and immediately killed 80,000 people; tens of thousands more would later die due to radiation exposure. Three days later, a second bomb was dropped on Nagasaki, killing an estimated forty thousand people.[12]

World War Two ended a month later, on 2 September 1945.

From 1941 to 1949, Doc Evatt (Herbert Vere Evatt, QC, PC, KStJ and Judge), when Australian Minister for External Affairs, played a significant role in shaping Australia's foreign policy. He was instrumental in the formation of the United Nations and in the foundation of the post-World War II international order. He was elected President of the General Assembly of the United Nations on 21 September 1948. Evatt presided over the assembly that adopted the *Universal Declaration of Human Rights* on 10 December 1948, the culmination of the work that he and his advisers had been doing since the emergence of proposals for a new world organisation during World War II.[13]

It was agreed that representatives of 50 countries meet to draw up a Charter for the proposed new *United Nations* (to replace the League of Nations). New UN headquarters were built specifically in New York, USA and occupied in 1952.

WILPF and the UN

WILPF was granted Consultative Status within the *UN Economic and Social Council* (ECOSOC) in 1948. WILPF has Special Consultative

Relations with the *United Nations Educational, Scientific and Cultural Organisation* (UNESCO) and the *United Nations Conference on Trade and Development* (UNCTAD), as well as special relations with the *International Labour Organisation* (ILO), *Food and Agriculture Organisation* (FAO), *United Nations Children's Fund* (UNICEF) and other organisations and agencies. WILPF's original office in Geneva, today organises specific UN conferences around human rights.

WILPF's second office in New York works closely with the United Nations. A special project named *Reaching Critical Will* works for disarmament and arms control of many different weapons systems, the reduction of global military spending and militarism, and the investigation of gendered aspects of the impact of weapons and of disarmament processes. This specialised disarmament project was set up by Australian WILPF woman, Felicity Hill.[14]

Interestingly, it was in 1947 that US President Franklin Roosevelt's wife, (Eleanor Roosevelt, a WILPF woman), suggested that the term 'rights of man' be changed to *human rights*. The term 'human right' was first coined by Thomas Paine and used in his English translation of the French *Declaration of Rights of Man and Citizen* (1789).[15]

WILPF Australia

In 1946, Doris Blackburn (wife of well-known Melbourne lawyer, Maurice Blackburn) was WILPF Australian President from 1928-1930. Her political career had begun in the *Women's Political Association*, and in 1946, she won the Federal seat of Bourke. She was also the first Victorian woman elected to Federal Parliament. Doris chaired the first *Ban the Bomb* meeting in Melbourne on the first anniversary of the Hiroshima bombings.

Doris Blackburn in her Parliamentary office

Blackburn forced debate in parliament on the establishment of the Woomera Rocket Range in central Australia on Aboriginal land. The following year, she was the only MP to speak against the Labor government's *Approved Defence Projects Bill* which imposed heavy penalties for public criticism on the project. She authorised a pamphlet on the *Rocket Range Menace* that threatens Aboriginal life. See more in Chapter three.

WILPF began calling for better conditions for Aboriginal people and this is explained more fully in the following chapters.

In 1952, WILPF had six Australian branches in Melbourne, Newcastle, Rockhampton, Sydney, Hobart, Perth and a study group in Adelaide.

In 1955, WILPF Victoria produced their *Remembering Hiroshima* flyer for their fortieth anniversary.

In 1956, WILPF produced a *Stop Nuclear Tests* flyer.

In 1962, WILPF formed an active branch in Adelaide, South Australia, campaigning about nuclear warfare and the Woomera Rocket

Range. Women also protested the transfer of West New Guinea to Indonesia.

In 1963 – WILPF Australia began opposition to the French nuclear tests in the Pacific. A WILPF woman, Jean Richards of NSW, flew to Paris to plead with President de Gaulle to stop the tests.

WILPF Anti-Nuclear Tests

In 1952, WILPF reformed a branch in Perth which became actively influential over the next fifty-five years. Irene Adelaide Greenwood (whose mother was from Adelaide) received many honours in recognition of her work for women through weekly ABC radio broadcasts over forty years where she promoted women's rights and peace. She worked with the Women's Service Guilds which included the feminist leader and Guilds' co-founder Bessie Rischbieth and Jessie Street (another famous women peace woman from Sydney NSW).

From 1948 until 1954 Greenwood hosted her women's radio session *Woman to Woman* from Perth, which considerably expanded her audience. She became President of the *Australian Federation of Women Voters*, State President (1966-69) of WILPF (WA) and edited their monthly peace journal *Peace and Freedom* for ten years.

Through these roles she was involved in WILPF's campaigning for nuclear and general disarmament and was scathing of Australia's continued export of uranium to countries with the potential to build nuclear weapons. As an Australian delegate, she attended the 1965 Golden Jubilee conference of WILPF in The Hague, Netherlands. She was an active participant in the protest movement against conscription and Australia's involvement in the Vietnam War.

In 1974, Prime Minister Gough Whitlam appointed Greenwood to the National Council for *International Women's Year*, 1975. She was appointed AO in 1975 and received a Queen Elizabeth II Silver Jubilee Medal (1977) and a United Nations Association of Australia Silver Peace Medal (1982). She was made a life member of the State Branch of the Fellowship of Australian Writers (1975), a life Vice President of the Women's Service Guilds of Western Australia and a life-Vice-President of the WA Branch of WILPF. In 1981, Murdoch University conferred on her an honorary doctorate. The WA government honoured her commitment to women and peace by naming its large coastal shipping vessel *Irene Greenwood* in 1982.

Ourselves and the Peril of Modern Warfare

What CAN we do in the face of it?
Remember Hiroshima! Everyone MUST act!

In common with many other people of the world, we must demand every possible protection of our RIGHT TO LIVE, and work to secure it IMMEDIATELY. Therefore we urge you to support the appeals to the World's Governments—and here in Australia, our appeal to the Commonwealth Government—to press for an emergency meeting of the United Nations Assembly, together with the representatives of all other existing Governments, including the Peoples' Government of China, to discuss the following steps towards a . . .

Security that does not depend on armed might!

(1) The immediate cessation of all experiments in destructive atomic explosions;
(2) The banning of production of all weapons of mass destruction;
(3) The scrapping of all existing stocks of such weapons;
(4) The guarantee of observance of (2) and (3) under supervision of a controlling body with representatives from both "East" and "West" and from neutral countries;
(5) The functioning of this body under the Security Council of UNO, to guarantee that atomic energy be used for peaceful purposes only;
(6) Compensation for damage caused by previous atomic testing;
(7) Pressure on all Governments to ratify the Geneva Convention banning chemical and bacteriological warfare, without reservation, and to establish an agreement regarding (1), (2) and (3) above;
(8) A Universal Declaration of Human Rights which would grant to PEOPLES the same protection against violence and exploitation that has long been recognised as needful for INDIVIDUALS;
(9) The development, under International Law, of a compulsory system of arbitration in cases of dispute between governments.

Issued by the Australian Section of the Women's International League for Peace and Freedom, 28 Thames Street, Box Hill, Victoria. This organisation has consultative status with UNO, UNESCO, ECOSOC, UNICEF, FAO, and is represented by Permanent Consultants at UN Headquarters and at Geneva.

June, 1955

40th ANNIVERSARY — 1915-1955

WILPF 40th Anniversary 'Remembering Hiroshima' flyer, 1955

STOP NUCLEAR TESTS!

OCTOBER, 1956

(From a statement issued by the 13th Triennial World Congress of the Women's International League for Peace and Freedom, held at Birmingham, England, in July, 1956. There were 200 delegates from eleven countries, including Australia. They included Members of Parliament, scientists, authors, doctors, lawyers, university professors and U.N. consultants.)

THESE WOMEN SAY:

"These experiments are an expression of suspicion and fear and the desire for military prestige. They promote and provoke competition in the manufacture of still more dangerous weapons of war.

They, like all other preparation for war, are a waste of money, materials and human effort that ought to be expended on the relief of suffering, want and ignorance.

They are a violation of human rights, since they cause and have caused distress to the Marshall Islanders and other unwilling and innocent victims.

On an immense scale, they cause suffering and death to animals, birds and fish exposed to their effects.

They contaminate international waters—without any international mandate.

They add, even if at present only a small amount, to the quantity of irradiation of every inhabitant of the world, with the consequent hazards to health of this and future generations, as recent official reports have pointed out.

Unless the Great Powers set an example, it will become more difficult at a later stage, to prevent an increase in the rate of such tests when other countries develop nuclear power stations and are able, if they wish, to develop nuclear weapons also.

An agreement to suspend further experiments would create a new atmosphere of hope and confidence and would prove to be a first step towards a genuine universal and total disarmament."

WHAT DO THESE TESTS MEAN?

OUR FOOD.—The Radiological Institute of Freiburg University (Germany) has announced that the level of radioactivity detected in some grain fields and pastures increased during July and August (1956) and reached a level, which, if maintained, *would be dangerous to humans.* The radioactivity was particularly serious on high ground; at about 4,000 feet it was ten times as strong as in the valleys. The *radioactivity of milk* from the grazing on the heights in the Black Forest was about five times as strong as that from the cows in the plains.

'Hydrogen Bomb' flyer, 1956

In 1963, WILPF began opposition to the French nuclear tests in the Pacific. A WILPF woman, Jean Richards of NSW, flew to Paris to plead with President de Gaulle to stop the tests. A Queensland branch was formed.

WOMEN
Say
French Perfume? YES!   French Bomb Tests? NO!

Let us join with women of America, Canada and many other countries in celebrating 1st November, as—

DEMAND DISARMAMENT DAY

Today, we want nuclear testing **everywhere**, by **anyone**, **stopped forever**. Yes, there has been a partial test ban, but **underground** testing has not stopped and preparations for the French Government's testing in the Pacific still go on.

THESE TESTS WILL DIRECTLY AFFECT US!

Scientists of international repute have warned us that with more radiation, bone cancer and leukemia will increase. More children are likely to be born without eyes and ears, or without arms and legs.

Mothers! Which do you fear more? The birth of physically or mentally defective children, or the new idea of social and economic planning for the prevention of war, and the determination to divert to peaceful purposes the enormous amount of money spent on war.

The "Herald", of July 29, 1963, carried a press report from Toronto —

NUCLEAR TESTS HIT CANADA
BABIES BORN CRIPPLED

"Heavy concentrations of deadly radioactive particles from Russian tests in the Arctic have doubled the number of deformed babies born in the Canadian midwest province of Alberta. The Canadian Medical Association in a report published in its weekly journal has warned that more deformed births can be expected. The study was ordered by Dr. Donovan Ross, the Alberta Minister for Health, when he noticed statistics showed a steady increase from 7.9 per thousand in 1959 to 13.8 per thousand in 1961 . . . Every type of deformity appeared with the same frequency among mothers who took no drugs as among those who did."

We all know that U.S.A., Great Britain and France have been involved in this poisoning of the atmosphere, too. Each release of poisonous material into the atmosphere makes our future a little more dangerous. Governments of Australia, New Zealand, Chili and Peru have objected to the forthcoming French tests, but individuals, too, must accept responsibility. THE FUTURE IS IN **YOUR** HANDS!

Governments of the world fear espionage and they fear deception but mothers rise above fear when their children's lives are at stake. The demand of our time is for intelligence, integrity and moral courage. Every one of us has **some** of each — let's use it. The task is not easy, but what we CAN do, we SHOULD do, we WILL do.

WILL YOU:
- **Write** to the French Consul, 34 Queen's Road, Melbourne and to your Federal Member (Mr. F. J. Davis, M.H.R., Mr. J. Jess, M.H.R., or whoever your member is), and tell them how you feel.
- **Talk** to your clergyman, your political party, your union, or your neighbour over the back fence.

WOMEN! YOUR POWER IS GREATER THAN YOU THINK!

For further information about "Women for Peace", contact:

Mrs. J. Hooke, 157 Canterbury Road, Blackburn. 89 2698.
Mrs. A. Walker, 100 Main Street, Blackburn. 89 1126.
Mrs. E. Harris, Centreway, Ringwood. ~~89 6036.~~ 87 6386

Reporter Print—89 6235   Authorised by A. Vroland, 28 Thames Street, Box Hill.

WILPF 'French Test' flyer

IT IS
CHEMICAL AND BIOLOGICAL WARFARE

CHEMICAL weapons are gases, liquids or dusts for <u>poisoning</u> humans, animals and vegetation.

BIOLOGICAL weapons are bacteria, viruses and similar agents for <u>deliberately causing disease</u> in humans, animals and vegetation.

The 1925 Geneva Protocol **PROHIBITED THEIR USE**, stating that they had been "justly condemned by the general opinion of the civilised world", and the Protocol was re-affirmed by the U.N. General Assembly in 1967. Australia acceded to it in 1930.

DO YOU KNOW THAT

CHEMICAL WEAPONS ARE BEING USED ALREADY ?

- **POISON GAS** has been used in the Yemen by the United Arab Republic.

- **"RIOT CONTROL" GAS** is being used in Vietnam by the U.S.A. and its allies — though described as non-lethal, it has killed one Australian soldier and countless old, young or sick Vietnamese.

- **DEFOLIANTS** are being used in Vietnam to destroy jungle cover and food crops; they are also toxic to animal life, may cause miscarriages in women, and scientists believe they will remain effective for many years, and may even render the soil itself sterile.

'Chemical and Biological Warfare' flyer

Steps of SA Parliament House, 'Nuclear Ban Treaty'
The Peace Museum

[1] www.foundingdocs.gopv.au 'Documenting a Democracy - An Act to provide for Uniform Federal Franchise'.

[2] Strong, Charles (?1844-1942) Entry in the *Australian Dictionary of Biography*, by C. R. Badger.

[3] Dr Charles Strong 'Pulpit and Platform' in *Commonweal* 1 Feb 1915, accessed SLC.186.

[4] Kate Laing, *Fighting for a New World Order: The Women's International League for Peace & Freedom 1915-1975*, p.29.

[5] *The Quest for Peace* by Eleanor Moore, p.41.

[6] Ibid.

[7] www.history.com/LeagueofNations

[8] *The Quest for Peace*, p.85.

[9] Ibid, p.91.

[10] Ibid, p.95.

[11] Ibid, p.94.

[12] www.Fromhistory.com .

[13] Ashley Hogan, *Moving in the Open Daylight; Doc Evatt, an Australian at the United Nations*, Sydney University Press.

[14] www.reachingcriticalwill.org

[15] www.hrlibrary.umn.edu

2

WILPF Forms a South Australian Branch

Global Context for WILPF SA Formation

It was unbelievable, but true, that after the huge number of people killed, and the destruction of so many cities during WW1 and WW2, the United States dropped nuclear bombs on the Japanese cities of Hiroshima on 6 August 1945 and Nagasaki on 9 August 1945. Peace groups now added anti-nuclear programs to their plans of work.

In 1962, there was a flashpoint moment between the United States and the Soviet Union which had initiated their ballistic missile deployment in Cuba. This 'standoff crisis' lasted for thirteen days, while the world held their breath that sanity would prevail. The reality of a potential nuclear bomb blast was brought home to everyone.

While Australia had been settled by the British and adopted many of their systems, after World War Two things began to change. Migrants and refugees, predominantly English, Italians and Greeks, settled in Adelaide. Slowly, people in Adelaide were learning about interesting cultures other than the dominant British, finding many commonalities.

In 1967, the Australian government held a Referendum to allow

Aboriginal people to be included in the census and to vote – this came back with a majority of 90.77 percent. This was a good step forward for better relations with the original inhabitants of the land we now shared together.

The United Kingdom of Great Britain and Northern Ireland joined the European Union on 1 January 1973, thus formally changing their dominant status as the British Empire which ruled the world, to focus on common issues with their close European neighbours.

America was on the rise toward becoming a dominant world power after the Cuban missile crisis. They wanted to shore up their pre-eminence by a worldwide network of military bases in friendly, aligned countries such as Australia. The next two decades saw key US/joint military installations placed in strategic places: Pine Gap (1966), North West Cape in WA (1974), Nurrungar in SA (1977) and Omega Base in Vic (1978). Pine Gap is one of the largest and most secretive US military intelligence gathering and communications bases outside America, thereby making it a prime target. These installations automatically brought Australia into the American sphere of influence should war break out.

These shifts in allegiance resulted in the Australian government's shift over time to support 'our great and powerful friend' beginning with Australian involvement in the Vietnam war in 1962. Australians now had television, so the violent deaths and destruction of Vietnam became well known, especially the footage of a young Vietnamese girl on fire, after a Napalm attack, fleeing her village. The use of phosphorous bombs and land mines also disturbed Australians and gradually changed their attitude toward Australian involvement in this war. The war lasted until 1975 with ever growing protests by Australians, not only opposed to conscription, but to the whole concept of war.

How can genuine peace and reconciliation ever result through the barrel of a gun?

Alongside this big change in allegiance, another movement from America spread to Australia – the women's liberation movement. The word 'sexism' was coined. By May 1970, the first nationwide conference on women's liberation was held in Melbourne – profiling 'female conditioning'. This concept quickly spread across Australia with key women leaders Germaine Greer's *The Female Eunuch* published in 1970, Dr Anne Summers' *Damned Whores and God's Police* in 1975, and Justice Elizabeth Evatt – the first female Judge of Australia's Family Court.[1]

The establishment of a women-only peace group was appealing and led to the establishment of a WILPF SA Branch which had local, state, national and international links.

WILPF SA BRANCH: 1952-1980

WILPF Australia already had active branches in Melbourne, Hobart, Sydney, Rockhampton and Perth for many years, all connected internationally through the Geneva office.

Despite being the first state to get the vote for women, our South Australian Branch was a late comer to WILPF. South Australia's prominent woman activist, Leonora Polkinghorne, led the League of Women Voters. She was also leader of the Housewives Association and the Union of Australian Women (SA Branch).

In 1953, the *WILPF South Australian branch* formed when the Women's Peace Crusade lapsed, following the death of its dynamic leader, Leonora Polkinghorne. Their members joined WILPF because of its national and international links. The SA Branch began as a study and reading group, with Eleanor Walker their secretary for many years.

Following the horrendous US nuclear bombings of Hiroshima and Nagasaki in Japan, the major powers turned their attention to making more deadly weapons – more nuclear bombs, chemical warfare and new spy bases all around the world.

It seemed that the race was now on to control and have power over others on a mega scale. The British used the Australian outback to test their nuclear weapons; and the French used their conquered land in the Pacific, Mururoa, for prolonged nuclear tests, all with disastrous contamination of both land, sea and people.

British nuclear tests were conducted in outback South Australia at Maralinga, between 1955 and 1963. Doris Blackburn, then WILPF Australian President, circulated her clever pamphlet *The Black and White of the Woomera Rocket Range*.

This era of nuclear madness has been somewhat reined in, but stockpiles of nuclear weapons still exist in scaringly huge numbers in United Kingdom, France, Russia, America, Israel and China. Peace activists worldwide called for them to be peacefully dismantled, so humanity can live in peace. It staggers the mind to think how the money spent on nuclear weapons design, testing and stockpiling, could have instead been used constructively, rather than for the potential total annihilation of specific areas.

The SA WILPF Branch urged our Australian Section to protest the transfer of West New Guinea to Indonesia and to ask the Australian government to investigate the activities of the Nazi Party in Australia. Peace education was also an integral part of SA Branch activities.

The SA Branch took on the secretariat of *WILPF Australian Section* (dealing with federal matters). WILPF also gave secretarial support to the newly formed *Aboriginal Women's Advancement League* based in Adelaide. Margaret Forte, WILPF's indefatigable Secretary, willingly took on these tasks with Mary McCrae, WILPF Aboriginal Liaison Officer. They also helped to organise and publicise two Aboriginal art exhibitions, one in the Llewellyn Galleries in 1970 and another in the Maitland District Hall in 1971.

Other like-minded local groups that WILPF networked with were - the *Global Education Centre*, the *United Nations Association of Australia*, the *Women's Electoral Lobby*, the *Union of Australian Women* and the *Women's Resource Centre*. Sadly, many of those groups have now disbanded for a variety of reasons. WILPF SA Branch continues today.

SA WILPF Campaigns

SA WILPF women campaigned on the apartheid system in South Africa that went from 1948-1994. 'This was a political and social system in South Africa during the era of White minority rule. Under this system, the people of South Africa were divided by their race and forced to live separately with laws in place to enforce segregation.'[2] (This concept of apartheid was adopted from an earlier Queensland Aborigines Act).

Opposing the system of apartheid became a world-wide struggle for peace and freedom. WILPF Australian National Secretary, Jennifer Fischhof, urged protest relating to South Africa 'as the only country in which discrimination is legal and constitutional. Boycotting of South African goods by Australian WILPF members dates from this year.'[3] This choice to boycott became a big issue for many Australians.

Apartheid did not end until 1994 when segregation was dismantled. African leader, Nelson Mandela, an anti-apartheid revolutionary and African political leader who had spent twenty-seven years in prison for opposing white rule, was released. The first free elections by the entire South African population were held. Mandela's long struggle for peace and freedom was rewarded when he became President of South Africa. This gave hope for a better, fairer world to many. WILPF women from the SA Branch had actively opposed apartheid and were pleased with this outcome after many years of activism.

In 1966, SA WILPF women interviewed candidates for the coming federal election. Prime Minister Harold Holt was returned with an increased majority.

WILPF organised an education weekend seminar at the University of Adelaide in October 1967, while continuing opposition to the Vietnam war.

In 1968, the WILPF SA branch hosted the second *WILPF National Section Conference* which was held at Mt Lofty, Adelaide, organised by the SA WILPF women who had developed a strong branch around the anti-Vietnam war issue. They elected their Executive Officers: Marjorie Ladkin as President, Maud McBriar as Vice President, Margaret Forte OAM as Secretary, Vera Tomkinson as Treasurer and Cynthia James as Librarian, archivist and merchandise person. This dedicated team worked diligently on the current issues of their time, not only locally, but nationally and internationally. They took over publishing the WILPF national bi-monthly *Peace & Freedom*, distributing to all WILPF branches in every state of Australia.

Maude McBriar OAM

Margaret Forte

The guest speaker at this 1968 conference was Mildred Scott Olmstead, Executive Director Emeritus of WILPF US Section. She was also a Quaker, and during WWI did international relief work with the *American Friends Service Committee* in France and Germany. She was also a member of the *American Association of University Women*, the *League of Women Voters*, the *Academy of Social Workers*, on the Board of the *Pennsylvania American Civil Liberties Union*, the *Martin Luther King Institute of Social Change*, the *Friends Peace Committee* and the *National Ghandi Centennial Committee*. She was one of a select group of American women who met with Soviet women at the *Soviet-American Women's Conference* arranged by WILPF at Bryn Mawr, Chicago, in 1961, and at the second meeting held in Moscow in 1964.

During 21-25 February 1969 – The *Human Rights Working Conference* was held at Canberra for NGOs with consultative status with the UN. Three WILPF women were chosen to represent their States – Betty King for WA, Maud McBriar for SA and Lorraine Moseley for NSW. The Conference called for:

- A Commission on the Status of Women;
- Commission on discrimination against Aborigines and minority groups;
- A Commission on Education and the Rights of the Child; and
- A Legal Commission.

The year 1969 saw a time of growth and achievement with the repeal of the National Service Act and the release of John Zarb (Vietnam War conscientious objector). WILPF produced a booklet *New Perversions of Science* which was distributed widely at the ANZAAS Conference and through the Adelaide University and Waite Research Institute mailing system to key academics.

WILPF SA Branch elected Janet Darling as their Vietnam War Campaign Coordinator (she was also a committed member of the SA *Save our Sons* women's campaign). The *Vietnam Moratorium March* on 18 September 1970, resulted in one of the worst exhibitions of conflict between police and public ever seen in South Australia. WILPF had well-defined views on the causes and consequences of the conflict and made a lengthy submission to the subsequent Royal Commission enquiring into this incident. The organisers of the march 'argued that street protest was a fundamental democratic right' and 'transnational solidarity is more important than the bond between State and citizen.'[4] WILPF women have always only carried out non-violent protest as we consider that violence in any form never solves the problem.

Other WILPF protests were marches and vigils outside the Federal Parliament Offices in No.1 King William Street, Adelaide. As mentioned, we had urged the release of John Zarb, a Victorian, who was the first conscientious objector to be imprisoned. Similar vigils and protests were also made on behalf of imprisoned South Australian conscientious objectors, especially Charles Martin, the only Australian conscientious objector to serve a full prison term. WILPF took part in a cavalcade of protest that travelled to the prison farm at Cadell while he was there and organised other protests.

The South Australian branch remembers with pride, when their Australian President, Betty Gale, was the key speaker at a *Peace March* through the streets of Adelaide, and the impressive speech she gave at the rally which followed. Betty had been invited to lead their SA march after her appearance on a nationally broadcast television discussion about the Vietnam War.

Speakers for the lunchtime meetings in April were Professor H Schiller on *The Slide to Violence in a Hungering World*; August- Professor K. Inglis on *New Guinea*; and in November, Judith Todd spoke on *Rhodesia*.

Guest speakers at other meetings that year were Mrs Mary Woodward, speaking on *The Right Sharing of the World's Resources*, Mrs Ann Barley on *Abortion Law Reform*; and Mr Peter Christianse on *Peaceful Uses of the Nuclear Explosions*. Other speakers over the year were: Mrs Joyce Clague who reported on the Aboriginal Conference held in Adelaide in June; Dr Marian Kent on the activities of European nations in the Middle East under the title *Oil and Empire*; Dr Neil Blewitt on *Australia's Foreign Policy*, and Ann McMenamin on *Peace and Politics*.

In 1971, WILPF SA branch undertook a major project for the year, the publication of a booklet on *The American Bases in Australia*. The main theme of the booklet was: *The only real nuclear deterrent is peace.*

Later, in 1973, WILPF initiated a submission asking the Prime Minister to honour the promise made in Adelaide on 31 July 1971, to expunge from the records all conscientious objectors' convictions made under the *National Service Act*. Another petition from this period asked the Government to review its interpretation of the *UN Declaration on Chemical and Biological Warfare*.

That same year, WILPF SA branch, as a member of the *Council Against Nuclear Testing*, was influential in getting the Council to widen their platform to include the need for international peace as another reason for opposing nuclear tests.

In the 1975 *International Women's Year* (IWY), WILPF branch was represented on the SA UN Committee for this event. Three sub-committees were set up to deal with *Equality, Development and Peace*. WILPF convened the Peace sub-committee, organising a seminar on *Handling Aggression* which was one of the biggest IWY meetings of the year. They also organised a luncheon talk by Charlotte Meacham on *Peace - the Neglected Issue of the IWY Conference in Mexico*. WILPF organised the publication of the papers of the Seminar (the only publication of the Committee).

With Gough Whitlam as Labor Prime Minister, the Australian government set up the *Australian National Advisory Committee (for women)*. WILPF members worked on IWY committees in their own States to strengthen the peace aim for the *UN Decade of Women*.

 **1975**

INTERNATIONAL WOMEN'S YEAR
AND 60TH BIRTHDAY OF
WOMEN'S INTERNATIONAL LEAGUE
FOR PEACE AND FREEDOM

THESE ARE THE AIMS OF I.W.Y.

(a) To promote EQUALITY between men and women
(b) To ensure the integration of women in the total DEVELOPMENT effort
(c) To recognise the importance of women's contribution to the development of friendly relations and co-operation among States and to the strengthening of world PEACE.

WILPF WORKS CONTINUOUSLY FOR I.W.Y. AIMS
NOT JUST THIS YEAR BUT EVERY YEAR

THESE ARE THE AIMS OF WILPF

(1) To bring together women determined to study, make known and help abolish the causes of war, and to work for a constructive peace
(2) To work for total and universal disarmament, peaceful settlement of all conflicts, and strengthening of U.N.O.
(3) To remove such restrictions on freedom as impair human dignity and to establish by non-violent means the conditions under which men and women may live in peace and justice, free from the fear of war and of want and of discrimination on grounds of sex, race, language, property, birth or other status, political, religious or other belief.

WHY NOT JOIN OUR ONGOING STRUGGLE FOR PEACE AND FREEDOM
Contact ~~Jennifer Neil 4672515 Margaret Holmes 9696755~~
Mrs. M. Waters, 10/21 Kensington Road, Sth. Yarra, 3141

International Women's Year, 1975

That same year, 1975, WILPF International President, Kay Camp (USA), visited Australia, spending a few days in each capital city. She told her Adelaide audiences at public meetings and on radio interviews about her recent trip to Chile to investigate conditions for women and children there. At this time, Chile had been ruled for two years by Pinochet's cruel, authoritarian military regime,[5] where over seventeen years many civilians were killed. This reminded us that WILPF is indeed an international, principled and fearless organisation which speaks truth to power!

Our national Australian Section also made several well-researched submissions to the *Ranger Uranium Environmental Inquiry 1975-1977*,[6] two of which were prepared in South Australia and presented at hearings held in Adelaide. These submissions included a long section on alternative energy sources and argued for a new approach to the basic needs and well-being of the world's people, and for a 'steady-state economy' in which energy consumption would be reduced, the wealth of the world shared more equitably, and a better basis found for international peace and security.

WILPF SA, Margaret Forte, with WILPF anti-uranium information stall

In 1975, WILPF women were thrilled when Molly Brannigan was one of two women chosen by the SA government to represent Australia at the *International Women's Year Conference* in Mexico.

In 1978, our WILPF Australian Section President, Margaret Holmes from the NSW branch went to Canberra to give evidence before the Joint Parliamentary Committee on *Foreign Affairs and Defence*, concerning our opposition to *Omega* installations in Australia. These were US global navigation systems based in Australia at several key places, including one in South Australia.[7]

The Australian Section became aware of the large number of political prisoners in Indonesia, many of them held for years without charges against them and reportedly living in terrible conditions. WILPF submissions were made urging the Australian government to protest to the Indonesian government. WILPF also supported and campaigned for human rights and political freedoms in East Timor.

In 1979, the *International Year of the Child*, the SA Branch organised and coordinated a lengthy three-part submission to the Prime Minister on the *Health, Education and Housing of Aboriginal Children*. WILPF carried out extensive research in all states for this submission.

Lunchtime talks relating to current affairs were a regular feature of WILPF SA's program. A highlight for WILPF was the visit by Hephzibah Menuhin, (sister of Yehudi Menuhin, the famous violinist). Hephzibah, not only accompanied her brother on the piano, but also was President of WILPF UK. She visited Adelaide and spoke to a packed Town Hall audience on 24 October 1979, about her work for human rights and her current campaign against *Torture, Torment and Terrorism*. She asked: 'What is the use of all the United Nations Covenants and Conventions on Human Rights when there are now over 70 dictatorships in the world, most of them using torture?'[8] Hephzibah called for an *International Tribunal for Accusation of Torturers and their Superiors*. Her visit generated much media interest.

Hephzibah Menuhin

Our Australian Section regularly questions federal election

candidates on matters relating to peace and defence. The SA branch always played its part in this and assisted in the framing of questions for all SA candidates for the 1980 elections.

The same year, WILPF was given $100 to offer as a prize for a peace song. With the help of other WILPF branches we organised this on a national basis and received entries from NSW, Victoria, Tasmania and South Australia. A recording of the winning song is sometimes still played.

WILPF SA Leaflets and Projects

During these years the SA branch produced leaflets on various topics:

In 1966, *No Conscripts for Vietnam* is based on a speech given by Dr JM Tregenza, a Senior Lecturer in History at the University of Adelaide.

A Way to Peace in Vietnam is a reprint of an article by Tich Nhat Hanh, a Buddhist monk who had visited Australia in 1965. It was produced to coincide with a visit to Australia by Air Vice Marshal Ky of South Vietnam.

In 1967, *Vietnam, A Matter of Conscience*, is a leaflet that included a letter to be sent to the Prime Minister (then Mr Holt) urging him to accept a three-point peace plan put forward by the Secretary-General of the United Nations, U Thant.

The National Service Act and Human Rights, is a leaflet that cited Articles 1, 2, 3, 12, 13, 18, 23 and 28 from the Universal Declaration of Human Rights, indicating how they were each contravened by the National Services Act.

1969 was a prolonged period of mega nuclear destruction of both environment and many life forms, WILPF produced a booklet *Perversions of Science* urging people to consider the new destructive 'perversion of science' behind the development of such weapons.

In 1972, *Igloo White* is an article that was reprinted from our WILPF American *Peace and Freedom* journal about the American electronic war system.

In 1973, *American Bases in Australia* was written. After 1973, the Vietnam war was no longer the major political issue. WILPF however, was still concerned about the restoration of Vietnam after the colossal damage it had suffered, and about the welfare of Vietnamese children, especially those with Australian fathers. In the early 1970s, Janet Darling (one of our original SA branch members), was Convenor of this project. She formed a *Committee of Responsibility for the Children of Vietnam* which sent money through a Quaker group to Vietnamese nuns who were caring for children. This project later continued through the *Red Cross* in Vietnam.

During 1979-1980 the problems of Australia's Aboriginal minority were ongoing concerns for WILPF. Our Australian Section President, Anna Vroland, called for human rights for Aborigines to be upheld. The SA Branch took over the secretariat for this campaign.

Two SA WILPF members, Mary McRae and Margaret Forte, coordinated WILPF's national project for the *UN Year of the Child*, sending a petition with more than 3,000 signatures to the Federal Parliament which called for better conditions and services for Aboriginal children.

In 1980, WILPF campaigned for protection of the Pitjantjatjara people from unrestricted mining on their land.

Nuclear-free Goals

French nuclear weapons testing occurred in the Pacific from 1966-1996. For 30 years[9] the French government undertook nuclear weapon tests in their Pacific Island territory, at Mururoa and Fangataufa. These tests were condemned internationally. WILPF women around the world urged France to desist in the destruction of the ocean, dependant life forms and local populations. Over this time, several huge international 'peace' convoys were sent to the area. A WILPF Sydney woman flew to France, (at her own expense) to ask President De Gaulle not to proceed with the testing, but he declined!

WILPF Australian women campaigned for nuclear-free zones in the Pacific Ocean.

WILPF women have always protested the establishment of the huge US Navy and Airforce base in Okinawa, Japan, which was established in 1951. It is still the focus of major Japanese and international peace groups today.

Meanwhile, SA WILPF women were concerned with a wide range of local issues – American bases, uranium mining, solidarity with indigenous people, peace education, discrimination on any ground, equality for women and many social justice issues. Women studied the facts so that they could speak out and work with those responsible for adjusting unfair or harsh policies.

WILPF Goals

SA WILPF goals reflect those of *WILPF International*:

- Universal disarmament under world law;
- Development of a world economic system for the benefit of all nations;
- A strengthened United Nations;
- Human and civil rights for all people; and
- Negotiation or arbitration of all conflicts.

WILPF Methods include:

- Research;
- Education;
- Publication of literature on non-violent solution of conflicts;
- Legislative lobbying; and
- Non-party political action.

WILPF women want peace among all people, as well as our government to respect everyone's right to a decent life, especially those who currently are marginalised. Yes, there is more work to be done!

[1] www.women Australia.info

[2] https://en.m.wikipedia.org/anti-apartheid movement.

[3] WILPF Section Profile Report, dated March 1980.

[4] 'Fighting against war – peace activism on the twentieth century' Edited by Phillip Deery and Julie Kimber, p.274.

[5] https://en.m.wikipedia.org Military Dictatorship of Chile 1973-1990).

[6] Commonwealth Governments Records about the Northern Territory, Part 2: Specific Issues 14 Environment-uranium mining – Ranger Uranium Environment Inquiry 1975-77 (records in the National Archives.naa.gov.au).

[7] Smh.com.au 'Cabinet papers 1992-93 Gippsland's Omega base made Australia a nuclear target' by Damien Murphy Dec 20, 2016 (date Cabinet papers were made public).

[8] Excerpt from Hephzhibah Menhuin's speech at Adelaide Town Hall, 24 October 1979.

[9] https://www.ctbto.org.frances nuclear testing programme.

3

First Nations Australians, the Settlement of South Australia, and WILPF's Campaigns to Seek Redress for Aboriginal Peoples

WILPF women Australia-wide support the full rights of Aboriginal people. We have consistently been concerned and active in bringing Aboriginal injustices to the notice of both State and Federal Governments and proposing reforms. We work cooperatively with Aboriginal groups in their campaigns for justice, peace and freedom.

Background to the Settlement of South Australia

In the late nineteenth and early twentieth centuries, social Darwinism and eugenics heavily influenced policy-makers who emphasised a racial vision of the world. Social Darwinists borrowed from Charles Darwin's theories of evolution in plants and animals and applied them inappropriately, to human societies. This assumed that Indigenous peoples were 'inferior races' who were doomed to fade away.

Most of the social policy implemented by the early Australian and State Governments or Protection Boards was motivated by this belief, which had the result of obscuring and erasing knowledge of Aboriginal culture. Alongside this, was the Christian belief that Aboriginal people would benefit from knowledge and love of God, thus becoming westernised.

However, soon after English settlers arrived in Australia, it became clear that Aboriginal people were not dying out. Despite the governing culture's belief that 'mixed race' people would no longer identify with the Aboriginal community, they found that they were instead identifying as Aboriginal, living with their Aboriginal relatives, and being identified by whites as Aboriginal. It was anxiety about assimilating categories of half castes into the dominant culture that led to the removal of 'mixed race children from their families' with the intention of separating them from their identification as Aboriginal.[1]

The Australian referendum in 1944 to give all rights to Aboriginal people failed.

In 1950, WILPF Australian President, Anna Vroland, took the Aboriginal issue to the Human Rights Commission of the United Nations. 'WILPF did not believe that white society was superior, just that the Aboriginal way of life was *different but not inferior and emphasised the need for special rights on account of the difference.*'[2]

In 1951, WILPF in Melbourne held a *Justice for Aborigines* meeting to raise their concerns. The South Australian branch commenced in 1952 and soon became actively engaged in supporting Aboriginal rights. WILPF nationally and through state branches, has seen 'Aboriginal equality and justice as an Australian issue of freedom'.[3] To better understand the context in which these various responses to Aboriginal people have evolved, it is pertinent to understand the early unique settlement of South Australia, first as an independent British colony, and later as a state of the Commonwealth of Australia.

Early Settlement in South Australia

SA Aboriginal right of legal occupation was contained in a unique SA document *Letters Patent* dated 19 February 1836, when the British colonists negotiated with King William IV, for the right to establish South Australia as a free colony. This document refutes the contention that South Australia was 'unoccupied.' The signed *Letters Patent* gave Aboriginal people *occupational rights on their tribal land* within the new State of South Australia. However, the early settlers set this agreement aside when they arrived here. Sadly, no real effort to learn the different Aboriginal tribes' traditional territories was ever seriously undertaken.

Governor John Hindmarsh, the first Governor of the new colony, showed an interest in the First Nations of the colony. He is recorded as commenting 'The local tribe, the Kaurna, seem friendly. Instead of being an ugly, stupid race, these are intelligent, handsome and active people.'[4]

Colonists simply bought or were granted land by their new government – thus dispossessing the original inhabitants of their traditional land without compensation. When Aboriginal peoples resisted their removal, sometimes waterholes and flour rations were poisoned, and massacres occurred. One year after the colonists' arrival, Matthew Moorhouse was appointed the first fulltime Protector of Aborigines to manage the situation, but dispossession and conflict continued.

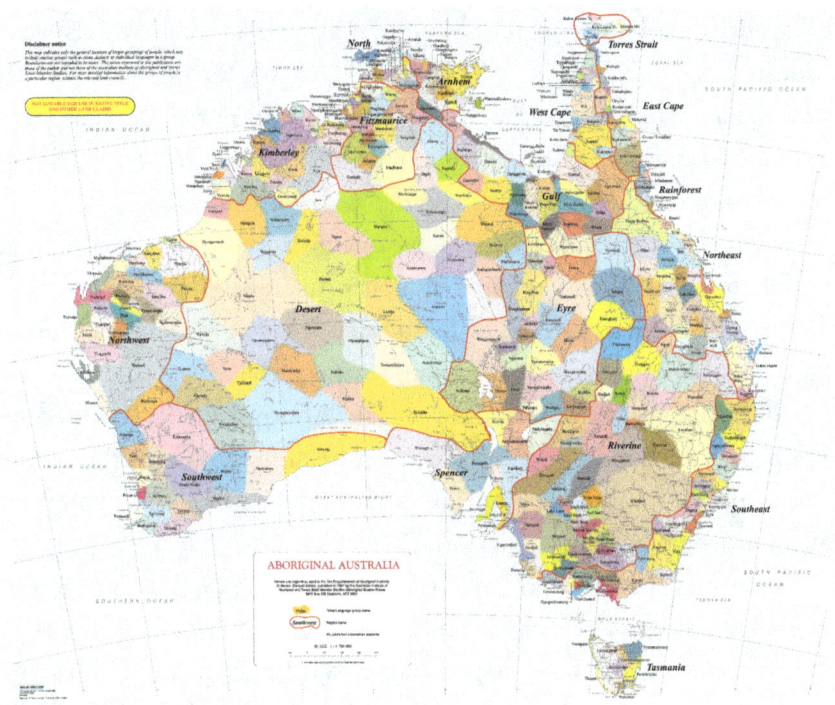

Aboriginal Language Map
Museums and Galleries of NSW

Aboriginal inhabitants today are still far from their earlier, pre-colonial right to enjoy their tribal land and culture. WILPF believes that Aboriginal people are entitled, and indeed were promised, rightful occupation and enjoyment of their tribal lands. We are aware that over recent years significant areas of Aboriginal traditional land have been returned to them. To fully understand our relations with First Nations peoples today, we need to be aware of their history of dispossession.

Forced Removal of Aboriginal children

From 1909 until 1968, the SA government had a policy of forced removal of mixed-race Aboriginal children from their families. Children's homes, such as 'Colebrook Home for Aboriginal Girls' in Eden Hills, were established across the state. Once children were admitted to these homes their parents could not reclaim them. Girls were educated and taught domestic duties so they could become domestic servants for white families. Some were trained as nurses, such as Lowitja O'Donoghue and Ruby Hammond in the 1950s. These mixed-race children were to become known as *The Stolen Generation*.

Gradually, the Aboriginal Department had total control of the welfare of all Aboriginal people in South Australia. Many were sent to delegated Aboriginal Reserves in country areas, for example to Point Pearce and Point McLeay (Raukkan). In 1939, the SA Aborigines Protection Board had power to allow certain Aboriginal people to receive an unconditional and/or limited exemption. The 1950s brought Assimilation policies, allowing Aborigines with 'mixed blood' to assimilate into the general white population.

Aboriginal people were affected by the British nuclear bomb tests at the Maralinga site (measuring 3,300 square kilometres) on their Tjarutja land in SA from 1956 to 1963. WILPF Australian President, Doris Blackburn wrote a stirring pamphlet condemning this bombing, entitled *The Black and White of the Woomera Rocket Range*. WILPF also put out a national flyer *A Call to the Women of Australia to Demand an Honourable Native Policy*.

THE BLACK AND WHITE OF THE ROCKET RANGE

One of the reasons why you are being asked to support the abandonment of the Central Australia rocket range proposal is that it is inimical to the welfare of the aborigines.

That is a good reason, but it is not the only one, or the most important.

Civilisation has brought death and degradation to Australia's aboriginal races. The immemorial hunting grounds of some of those who manage to exist are to be invaded by a civilisation intent on bringing death and destruction on itself.

So that the master races may discover how to destroy each other more efficiently, the subject races are to suffer. Much can be said of the effect of the rocket range on the natives—but what of its effects on their dispossessors?

The victors in the Second World War have set up an organisation dedicated to the prevention of war and "the maintenance of international peace and security." At least one of them has the atomic bomb. Another —Australia—is to be the testing ground for rockets. Put those two weapons together, and mankind has the greatest danger to itself that it has ever invented.

The weapons to be tested are literally and essentially indiscriminate. The authority for that statement is Mr. Churchill. He said it when the Germans alone held their secret. Lord Croft, then Under-Secretary for War, spoke of "foul, indiscriminate murder by flying-bombs."

The V2 rocket was worse. Australia is now going to play a part in evolving still worse methods of "foul, indiscriminate slaughter."

Professor Oliphant, one of the founding fathers of the atomic bomb, has said that mankind must renounce war or commit suicide. Dozens of other leaders have said much the same thing. Australia is to help to produce the weapons—essentially aggressive weapons—for the war in which mankind is to commit suicide.

How will other nations regard this? Will they look upon it as a peaceful act? Will they mark down Australian cities as priority targets when the atomic bombs and the rockets begin to fly?

What do you think? What would you think if you lived in one of those other countries?

The rocket range plan should be abandoned now, not only because it is a danger to the aboriginal way of life, but because—

It is a danger to peace and to Australia.

It is an incitement to potential enemies.

It is incompatible with the spirit of the United Nations' Charter.

The Black and White of the Rocket Range
Victorian pamphlet

Political and Legal Changes

By 1962, the SA Government passed the *Aboriginal Affairs Act* which removed all restrictions on Aboriginal people. Don Dunstan was appointed Minister for Aboriginal Affairs and was at the forefront of the Labor Party abandoning the *White Australia Policy*.

The 1966 *Wave Hill Walk-Off* by Northern Territory Aboriginal stockmen, protesting their low wages, poor conditions and disrespectful treatment over a century of servitude, gained national television coverage of the injustices Aboriginal people had faced.

In 1975, Prime Minister, Gough Whitlam transferred leasehold title to the Gurindji people. He symbolically placed a handful of red soil into Vincent Lingiari's hand. This event spurred on the handing over of land to traditional owners nationally.

The nationwide *Referendum for Constitutional Reform* was passed in 1967. It legally recognised Aboriginal people as Australian citizens with the right to vote. Ninety percent of voters said *YES*.

The 1988 *South Australian Aboriginal Heritage Act* gave statutory protection and preservation of Aboriginal heritage, but this is separate to native title.

Since that time, various other Acts have been passed to give Aboriginal people more rights and respect. Despite the 1990 *Royal Commission into Aboriginal Deaths in Custody*, the high number of deaths continue.

That same year, the Commonwealth government established the *Aboriginal and Torres Strait Islander Commission* (ATSIC) which took over much responsibility for Aboriginal Affairs and Health. Lowitja O'Donoghue AC, CBE, DSG (the young Aboriginal girl placed in Colebrook Home in SA) was the inaugural ATSIC Chairperson. She received many honours for her work. ATSIC was dismantled in 2004 under Prime Minister, John Howard, who proposed selecting indigenous people to advise the government as required. Aboriginal specific programs were then mainstreamed under the control of existing

Commonwealth Departments. This change was highly contested and remains a divisive issue.

The 1992 *Mabo vs. Queensland (No.2) High Court Decision* (known as the *Mabo Decision*) is of great significance. The famous Eddie Mabo case which lasted for eight years, gave legal recognition of traditional *Native Title* rights to Aboriginals and overturned the concept that Australia was *terra nullius* (empty land).

In 1996, *The Wik Judgement of the High Court* found that pastoral leases did not necessarily extinguish Native Title and that both could co-exist, but where there are conflicts, Native Title rights are subordinate to the rights of the pastoral leaseholder.

During 1997, there was the *National Enquiry into the Separation of Aboriginal and Torres Strait Islander Children* from their families. The *Bringing Them Home* report was launched, recommending Premiers and the Prime Minister apologise for the wrongdoings of the past, which all State Premiers did immediately, however, then Prime Minister John Howard, did not.

In 2008, on 13 February, then Prime Minister, Kevin Rudd, moved a formal motion of *Apology to Indigenous Australians*, acknowledging that government policies 'had inflicted profound grief, suffering and loss on these our fellow Australians.'[5] Since that time, other laws have been passed to address the various obstacles that Aboriginal people still face today.

Aboriginal delegates held a *First Nations National Constitutional Convention* which met over four days in May 2017 at Uluru. They called for a *First Nations Voice* in the Australian Constitution and a *Makarrata*[6] which means coming together, working together and making peace together. In 2017, the *Uluru Statement from the Heart*[7] was supported by Aboriginal peoples at the 2017 National Constitutional Convention and a *Makarrata Commission* formed to oversee a national process for Treaty and Truth-Telling, as the way forward toward genuine reconciliation.

Indigenous Australians want Constitutional recognition. Despite overwhelming national support from many Australians, the Liberal Governments of Tony Abbott, Malcolm Turnbull and Scott Morrison refused to support their request for formal recognition. The Labor Government, led by Prime Minister Anthony Albanese from 2022, is committed to implement the *Uluru Statement from the Heart* in full.

WILPF women support the Uluru Statement and call for its implementation, including granting a First Nations' Voice for Aboriginal and Torres Strait Islanders to be enshrined in the Constitution.

Uluru Statement of the Heart wins the Sydney Peace Prize, 2021

WILPF SA's Support of Aboriginal Rights

In the 1960s and early 1970s, WILPF women in their SA Branch (established in the 1950s), helped with many Aboriginal activities, particularly assisting to establish and support the *Council for Aboriginal Women and the Aboriginal Legal Rights Movement*, with Manager, Ruby Hammond. WILPF woman, Margaret Forte, took on the secretarial work for the Council for Aboriginal Women and later wrote a biography of Ruby Hammond's Aboriginal activism over many years until her death in 1993, titled *Flight of an Eagle*.

WILPF women were particularly active in promoting the *Yes* vote for the Aboriginal question in the 1967 Referendum. This Referendum was called by the Harold Holt Liberal Government on 27 May 1967 with the first part asking for 'Aboriginal people to be counted in the Australian census and asking the government to legislate separately for Aboriginal people.'[8] WILPF women also helped to organise and publicise two Aboriginal art exhibitions, first at the Llewellyn Galleries, Adelaide University in 1970, and then at the Maitland District Hall in 1971.

In the 1970s, WILPF made a conscious decision to work with other non-Aboriginal groups in support of reconciliation, so they could make the wider community aware of the discrimination and disadvantage to which the Aboriginal people were, and are, continually subjected.

SA WILPF woman Dr Bev Hall, with husband Ron, took their young family to Canada to learn more about education programmes in First Nations communities there, and to study Intercultural Education. Canada appeared to have a more enlightened view than Australia towards its Indigenous peoples. Bev and Ron had both been involved with the SA Aboriginal Advancement League with campaigns for Aboriginal human rights in South Australia, for five years prior to leaving. They hoped to learn more to bring about greater understanding between Indigenous and non-Indigenous people. However, they also learnt about how mining companies were deceiving the communities and seizing resources despite treaties, which the local Indigenous communities did not benefit from.

In 1979, for the *International Year of the Child*, WILPF's project was a three-part open submission to the Prime Minister on the *Education, Health and Housing of Aboriginal Children*. WILPF women presented this report to the then Prime Minister, Malcolm Fraser, on World Health Day, 7 April 1979, then again on National Aborigines Day, 13 July 1979, and again on United Nations Day, 24 October 1979.

In the 1980s, an *Aboriginal Land Rights Support Group* was set up in Adelaide to assist the Pitjantjatjara and Yankuntyjara peoples in the north-west of South Australia in their campaign for title to land they regarded as theirs for many thousands of years. WILPF joined this group and actively supported it. Mary McCrae, WILPF Branch *Aboriginal Liaison Officer*, and her sister, Marjory Thomas, gave many hours to helping the Aboriginal people put their case to the then SA Premier, David Tonkin. WILPF helped with transport and assistance to camp on the Victoria Park racecourse by providing tents and cooking equipment. WILPF worked together with other groups to prepare a submission to the State Government.

In November 1981, the David Tonkin Liberal Government amended the SA Labor Premier Don Dunstan's Government's *SA Aboriginal Land Rights Act* 1978. Tonkin travelled to Itjinpirie Creek, just north of Ernabella, to hand over an inalienable freehold title to 102,360 square kilometres of land to the Pitjantjatjara and Yankunytjatjara people.

Although *reconciliation* was not a word in circulation in 1981, WILPF saw and still sees this as an example of what can be achieved by a positive, non-aggressive campaign.

In 1984, Labor Premier John Bannon's government passed legislation to return land to the Maralinga Tjarutja people.

Australia's Bicentennial Year was in 1988. Another WILPF project was to seek employment opportunities for Aborigines, especially young people. WILPF members wrote to department stores, insurance companies and banks, suggesting they find employment on their staff for young Aborigines. WILPF followed this project throughout the year but were disappointed with the results. Replies indicated that employers selected staff on their perceived merits and would employ Aborigines only if they seemed the most suitable. The idea of special training was never commented on.

During 1990 -2001, in SA, the *Hindmarsh Island Bridge* controversy caused considerable pain for the women involved. These were also the years in which the struggle to protect the rights of the Ngarrindjeri women on Kumerangk (Hindmarsh Island) developed. The Indigenous women objected to a bridge being built to link the island to the mainland because of spiritual and cultural factors in relation to beliefs that are sacred to those women. WILPF women travelled many times to Goolwa to be present at protests and to keep in touch with the Aboriginal Heritage Support Group.

WILPF joined with *Women's Electoral Lobby* in objecting to the State Government about the Hindmarsh Island bridge, about which the groups felt outrage, disgrace and shame as South Australian women. WILPF also made a submission to the Royal Commission investigating this whole affair. WILPF supported Dr Deane Fergie and Professor Cheryl Saunders who supported the Ngarrindjeri women and were being sued for $70 million by the Chapmans, the proposed developers. The Court ruled in favour of the applicants, saying they believed Aboriginal women's spiritual connection to that area was fabricated. Aboriginal Elder, Veronica Brodie, who had testified, was supported by WILPF women.

National Reconciliation

Reconciliation Australia, the lead body for reconciliation in Australia, write that 'reconciliation is about strengthening relationships between Aboriginal and Torres Strait Islander peoples and non-Indigenous peoples, for the benefit of all Australians.' They suggest that 'reconciliation is based and measured in five dimensions: historical acceptance; race relations; equality and equity; institutional integrity; and unity.'[9]

In 1991 the Federal Parliament passed the *Council for Aboriginal Reconciliation Act* presented by the then Labor Aboriginal Affairs Minister, Robert Tickner. It was passed unanimously with a rare show of bipartisan support. The Council was established after the *Royal Commission into Deaths in Custody* recommended that a formal and ongoing process of reconciliation between Indigenous and non-Indigenous Australians should begin. Parliament said at that time that it was 'most desirable that there be such a reconciliation' by 2001, the year in which Australia would celebrate its centenary of Federation.

The following year, 1992, two important events brought the process of reconciliation forward. First, the High Court of Australia brought down a decision in the historic *Mabo* case in which it rejected the fallacy of *terra nullius* (that Australia had belonged to no one at the time of European invasion in 1788) as justification for ignoring traditional Indigenous property rights.

Second, in December of that year, then Labor Prime Minister, Paul Keating, said in a speech at the launch of the *International Year of the*

World's Indigenous People at Redfern, NSW, that white Australia had failed Indigenous Australians: 'We committed the murders. We took the children from their mothers. It was our ignorance and prejudice.' He promised to redress past wrongs and that the government would respond to the Mabo decision.

In 1993, Parliament passed the native title legislation.

The Liberal Party was elected to Federal Parliament with John Howard as Prime Minister in 1996. In April 1997, The *National Inquiry into the Separation of Aboriginal and Torres Strait Islander Children from their Families* produced the report *Bringing Them Home*. The report concluded that forcible removal of children from their families was an act of genocide, contrary to the *Convention on Genocide* ratified by Australia in 1949 and recommended that the government formally apologise to the stolen generations.

The *Council for Aboriginal Reconciliation* held its first national convention in May that year. The delegates at the convention turned their backs on Prime Minister Howard because he rejected making a formal apology on the basis that *'Australians of this generation should not be required to accept guilt and blame for past actions and policies.'* This was a blow for the reconciliation process.

It was a momentous occasion for all Australians when, on 13 February 2008, then Labor Prime Minister, Kevin Rudd, made a formal apology to the *Stolen Generation* in Federal Parliament. This event was met by overwhelming joy, by both the Aboriginal people who had endured so much discrimination, as well as the people of Australia who overwhelmingly supported this gesture of goodwill and reconciliation.

Pool of Tears monument, Blackwood, remembers the grief of the families of Aboriginal and Torres Strait Islander children taken away in forcible removal.

Sculptor Silvio Apponyi, assisted by Kaurna sculptor Sherren Rankine and Yankunjatjara artists Tjula Jane Pole and Kunya June-Anne McInerney

SA WILPF's Contribution to Work for Reconciliation

In 1993, the *International Year for the World's Indigenous People* was declared. SA WILPF's project this year was the biggest they had ever undertaken. It was designed to reach school children and to encourage them to think of the past and the future *Through Aboriginal Eyes*. WILPF promoted an art competition for an extensive exhibition which was exhibited throughout the year at Tandanya, SA's National Aboriginal Cultural Institute, for a month from 4 August to 4 September; then at the State Bank from 11-29 October; and then in the Education Department Art Gallery from 1-12 November. Thirty schools participated and the three exhibitions attracted a great deal of attention and publicity.

It was within this context that Léonie Ebert, a long time SA WILPF woman, also on the Board of the Graham F Smith Peace Trust Inc., decided in late 1997 to make a contribution to the people's push for reconciliation through a *Peace Trust*. She asked the Trust to collaborate with the Kaurna people and design appropriate artwork to adorn the forecourt of the Adelaide Festival Centre. The installed artwork consists of a seven-metre piece of simple sculptural forms, which represent the historical legacy and cultural heritage of the Kaurna people. There is a centrally placed sculpture representing Kaurna spiritual beliefs in moving water, surrounded by four bold minimalist rock formations. A Project-Walking Trail Guide explains the symbolism.

Elements of this artwork symbolise the great sky river *Wodliparri* (literally 'hut river', commonly known as Milky Way) and the *Yurakauwe* (a lagoon in the dark parts of *Wodliparri*, belonging to the giant serpent, *Yura*). *Wodliparri* was so named because *Kaurna meyunna* believe the bright stars on the edge to be the campfires of ancestors along the edge of their river in the sky world. The sky world reflects life on earth. Life sustaining fresh water is central to meeting places on earth and spiritually in the sky world — past, present and in the future. For some people today, the water might also represent tears linked to the reconciliation process. Spiritual links between the heavens and the earth of all peoples can be pondered since we all share the changing night sky and require fresh water to sustain life. The sculptured shield is a symbol for *Kaurna meyunna*, representing the past, the present and future.

The monumental artwork created and installed by Tony Rosella, Darren Siwes and Eileen Karpany and sculpted by Donato Rosella, followed a lengthy consultative process with Aboriginal people and organisations. In acknowledgment of *Reconciliation and Peace*, the artwork explores some of the Kaurna history in the context of events, experiences and spiritual meanings. The sculptures communicate this story visually, powerfully and sensitively.

In March 2001, Trish Worth, former MP for Adelaide, launched this *Kaurna Reconciliation* artwork at the Adelaide Festival Centre. WILPF woman Léonie Ebert is to be thanked for her vision and effort to make a tangible reconciliation monument for all Australians to reflect upon.

In 1997, a *WILPF Reconciliation Sub-committee* was formed. WILPF women actively supported and attended many meetings held in Adelaide, leading up to the *National Reconciliation Convention* held in

Melbourne on 26 to 28 May. WILPF organised their own reconciliation meeting at Tandanya on April 28, to which they invited women from Camp Coorong and other parts of the state. It was a very warm and successful meeting with about 70 women present, half of them Aboriginal. From this meeting, WILPF sent a message to the national Convention. During the evening, an award was presented to the Aboriginal women of South Australia in recognition of their struggle for rightful justice, peace, freedom and equality.

In 1998, WILPF SA branch researched and wrote an extensive document, *Native Title: A background paper prepared by WILPF SA Branch*. It traces the relations with white people from Captain Cook, the newly established settlement of South Australia and to the current day, outlining the changes in attitude and support for Aboriginal people over the last two hundred years. This stands as an excellent historical research and report.

From 1998-2004 the Australian government proposed a nuclear waste dump in South Australia.

> In 2003, the Federal Government used the Lands Acquisition Act 1989 to seize land for the dump. Native Title rights and interests were extinguished with the stroke of a pen. This took place with no forewarning and no consultation with the Aboriginal people.[10]

WILPF women supported the *Kupa Piti Kungka Tjuta* women's opposition to this nuclear waste dump near Coober Pedy. Several women went to the Aboriginal women's camp in solidarity and gave regular support through the six years of this campaign. A Federal Court challenge from the South Australian Government finally put an end to the dump.

From 2006-2007, WILPF women supported Aboriginal Elder, Veronica Brodie's wish to have the disused Port Adelaide Flour Mill become an *Aboriginal Heritage Centre*. Sadly, this was refused by the SA Liberal government. Veronica's health failed and when she was close to dying,

WILPF woman Sue Gilbey went regularly to the early morning market to get fresh *bony bream* fish from Veronica's beloved Coorong, to take and cook for Veronica, as this was her dying wish!

WILPF invited Aboriginal woman, Lilian Holt, to co-present with our SA Coordinator, Cathy Picone, a workshop on *Why Whiteness?* on 3 March 2008. This was very informative and sometimes confronting, when comparing the privileges that being 'white' gave us, while denying those same privileges to Aboriginal people.

The Federal Government proposed a nuclear dump on the Muckaty Aboriginal land in the Northern Territory. WILPF women supported the NT *Muckaty*[11] Aboriginal women's successful campaign from 2010-2014, until it was stopped. One of our actions was to hold a photographic exhibition in Adelaide during *The Fringe* with invited Muckaty Aboriginal Elders to speak at the opening of our exhibition.

The 2020 WILPF campaign supports the local SA Aboriginals' wish to stop a nuclear waste dump being built in South Australia, at Napandee, near Kimba. There are still many health, discrimination, housing and education issues facing Aboriginal communities, despite a *Stronger Futures* document passed in the Senate in 2013 and a National Aboriginal and Torres Strait Health Plan developed for 2013-2023.

Summary

WILPF women have always been acutely aware of the injustices Aboriginal people have endured. We understand the simple concept of 'power over' as injustice, to 'power with' as equality and respect. Our SA branch has run specific programmes to explore this concept – such as Cathy Picone's excellent workshops, exploring the privileges of 'whiteness' in the 1990s.

Over time, SA WILPF women have also been members of other organisations such as the *Aboriginal Advancement League*, the *Aboriginal Legal Rights Movement* (ALRM) and *Australians for Native Title and*

Reconciliation (ANTaR) which is a national movement of Australians in support of justice, rights and respect for Australia's First Peoples.[12]

Currently, we are working with Aboriginal women at Parafield Gardens to improve conditions and outcomes for women caught in our women's prison system with little support, while incarcerated, and when they are released.

These are just some of our stories of WILPF women working at all levels to publicly expose injustice and violence, ranging from small, personal indignities to involvement in British and American wars.

SA WILPF women work to bring justice to Indigenous peoples as the need arises. We work at the personal, local, state and national levels to offer our support when Aboriginal leaders ask for it, as we want everyone to live in a just and equal society. We have some way to go yet to achieve this and ask everyone to consider what they can do to make Australia truly a place of peace and freedom for all.

[1] 'Aboriginal Rights', Kate Laing PhD thesis *Fight for a New World Order: The Women's International League for Peace & Freedom in Australia 1915-1975*. Latrobe University Melbourne June 2017, p. 5.

[2] Ibid, p.178

[3] WILPF SA Branch report, 'SA Branch Aboriginal Support,' Margaret Forte, 1997 (copy in WILPF SA Branch archives).

[4] *Australian Origins to Eureka*, Thomas Kenneally, Allen & Unwin, 2009, p.293.

[5] National Sorry Day.

[6] SA Health Aboriginal Health Plan and History Timeline compiled from SA Department of Health.

[7] Uluru Statement from the Heart released on 26 May 2017.

[8] www.wikipedia.org/wiki/1967_Australian_Referendum (Aboriginals)

[9] https://www.reconciliation.org.au/reconciliation/

[10] www.foe.org.au/radioactive-waste-and-nuclear-war-australias-aboriginal-people

[11] www.beyondnuclearinitiative.com
[12] www.antar.org.au

4

WILPF SA's Involvement in the Vietnam War, 1962-1972

Background to the Australian Involvement in the Vietnam War

Australia's interest in Southeast Asia and the Federal Government's support for American foreign policy in this area soon lead to military involvement in South Vietnam, just as the civil war in Korea had resulted in the sending of Australian troops to support the South against the North in the early 1950s.

In 1954, the Republic of Vietnam had been proclaimed after the French, who had colonised Vietnam a hundred years earlier, and had been defeated at Dien Bien Phu by the Viet Minh forces led by Ho Chi Minh. Independence for Vietnam had been guaranteed by the Geneva Agreement in which fourteen nations took part. One provision of the Agreement was that Vietnam should be divided at the seventeenth parallel between North and South Vietnam until elections could be held in 1956. The United States had not signed the agreement but had agreed to refrain from the use or threat of use of force. Dinh Diem, former Prime Minister of Vietnam, remained in power in South Vietnam until his assassination in 1963, while in 1956, the North held elections, giving full support to Ho Chi Minh and the Communist Party of Vietnam.

The United States began bombing North Vietnam in August 1954, after the Bay of Tonkin incident, where there were clashes between the torpedo boats of Hanoi's navy and US Navy destroyers. This incident had been provoked by America's clandestine raids on economic and military targets in North Vietnam, but this did not prevent then US President Lyndon Baines Johnson from using the situation to escalate the war.[1]

'From 1954 Communist North Vietnam and South Vietnam were at war. In the 1960s, hundreds of thousands of US troops were involved in support of South Vietnam and the Australian Government also decided to commit 50,000 troops.'[2] Australian support for US foreign policies, in the Cold War climate of the time, rested on fear of China and Vietnam becoming the frontier against Chinese expansion. This 'domino theory' was promoted by the then Prime Minister Robert Menzies' Liberal Government. This geopolitical theory implied that the fall of a non-communist state to communism would prompt the fall of neighbouring states.

Conscription for Australian 20-year-old Males

On 10 November 1964, a bill to introduce conscription of twenty-year old males for overseas service was introduced. Forewarned, a delegation of various women's groups, including WILPF, lobbied Ministers and Members of Parliament, appealing to them to vote against the Bill. Thousands of *No Conscription* cards were posted to the Prime Minister.

Earlier, at an election in Hornsby, the Sydney branch of Women's International League for Peace and Freedom organised a vigil of women wearing black sashes to stand silently, while Prime Minister Menzies spoke. Branches held regular vigils against the war. The Victorian branch held a weekly vigil for five years outside the Victorian State Library in Swanston Street.

NSW WILPF Vigil

Debbie Knopman from the Waverley Branch of the Union of Australian Women who also took part in the protest wrote:

> The idea was to have a silent vigil as a protest, with about 30 women participating, standing with black veils over their heads, when given the signal to do so in the middle of the Prime Minister's speech. The *Sydney Morning Herald*, the next day, reported in their front-page article that:

> 'Women in black hoods fail to shake Menzies at Poll Rally'. As one who attended, I can vouch for the fact that it just about stopped him in his tracks. The packed hall turned to see the cause of the disturbance, surely getting the protest message.[3]

Despite opposition from many quarters the Bill was passed, including a clause that conscripts were to be selected based on their birthday being drawn from a barrel. This Act, more than any other, incensed and aroused a wide section of the population. The Labor Party too changed its stand when an infantry battalion was committed to Vietnam in 1965, it united in its opposition to the new Act.[4]

The objective was 'to support South Vietnam against Communist attacks from North Vietnam. The estimated cost of Australia's involvement in this war was $218.4 million.'[5]

Australian Prime Minister, Menzies, introduced a new *National Service Act* of 1964 which required men, selected by ballot birthdays, to serve two years in regular Army units, followed by a further three years on the active reserve list. In May 1965, the Defence Act was amended to provide that these conscripts could also be required to serve overseas.

Many young men refused to register and were supported by citizens opposed to conscription. Two SA conscientious objectors were arrested for refusing to register – John Zarb and Robert Martin – and both were jailed. [6] SA WILPF women actively opposed their imprisonment and campaigned for their release throughout the whole war.

From 1965 to 1972 when the last Australian troops were withdrawn from Vietnam, over 800,000 men were registered for National Service, 63,000 conscripted by the ballot. During that time, 15,381 national service men served in the Vietnam war, with 200 killed and 1,279 wounded.[7] This war was the cause of the greatest social and political dissent in Australia since the conscription referendums of WW1.[8] National Service continued until 1972, when the newly elected Gough Whitlam Labor Government suspended it.[9]

Many Australians were opposed to involvement in the Vietnam war and even more objected to the use of conscripts there. The first conscript to die was a South Australian, Ervol Noack.

SA WILPF's Opposition to the Vietnam War

From 1965, SA WILPF women's work was dominated by opposition to the Vietnam war. WILPF women made banners and joined in the first of many anti-Vietnam war marches in Adelaide. In March 1966, while the then Prime Minister, Harold Holt, was in Adelaide, WILPF women organised a protest march from Victoria Square to the South Australian Hotel on North Terrace where he was staying. This was the first anti-Vietnam march to be held in Adelaide.

WILPF women marching

WILPF women after marching

WILPF women have always been proud of their prompt initiative to opposing war.

Cynthia James with
her 1968 banner

Rita Shortland with
her 1968 banner

Soon, a *Campaign for Peace in Vietnam*, a group for both men and women, was formed. WILPF SA member, Sylvia Duckhouse, became its secretary, with WILPF branch members always supportive of and involved in the Campaign's activities. They campaigned vigorously against conscription and thousands joined their protest marches in Adelaide. Many young men refused to register and were supported by citizens opposed to conscription. Simultaneously, WILPF women also carried on regular branch activities, including deputations to Members of Parliament on a range of issues, as well as ongoing support for conscientious objectors.

Campaign for Peace in Vietnam
State Library of SA

SA Anti-Vietnam rally, Rundle Mall

In 1965, the 50*th* *Anniversary Congress of WILPF* was held at The Hague in the Netherlands. The Congress decided to initiate an *Appeal* to *American Women to Help Stop the War in Vietnam*. Lorraine Moseley, on behalf of WILPF Australian Section, accepted the onerous task of international co-ordinator, collecting signatures to the Appeal from many of the world's leading women.

The work of this Appeal continued in South Australia. Regular protests and street marches continued. This reply was received from the Adelaide City Council about a proposed anti-Vietnam War march. It stated:

> I acknowledge your letter of 19 July 1969 and in reply you are advised that in so far as the Adelaide City Council is concerned, permission is granted to your League to stage a street march on Saturday, 2 August 1969.
>
> Those taking part in the event are to assemble in Victoria Square and move from there at 10.30am and proceed to Elder Park via the western footpaths of King William Street and King William Road, in single file obeying traffic signals. On reaching the AMP building, corner King William Street and North Terrace, marchers may halt momentarily while a small deputation enters the building to take up to the Federal Parliamentary offices a Petition to the House of Representatives for the repeal of the National Service Act and the release of John Zarb.
>
> Should placards and banners be carried, they may only be made of calico or cardboard and not exceeding 1/32 inches in thickness, must be held in the hand and not supported by any framework or poles. Bills and posters may not be affixed to lighting poles and buildings etc.
>
> On Monday, 4 August 1969, permission is granted to mount, from 9am to 5pm, a silent vigil of two women, standing one each side of the King William Street entrance to the AMP building, each holding

a 'Release Zarb' placard. The above-mentioned conditions in relation to placards and banners etc. also apply to this vigil.

The Commissioner of Police has been advised and any requests from his Officers or Corporation Officers should be complied with immediately. Yours faithfully, (signed) RW Arland Town Clerk.

ASIO file photo of a SA anti-Vietnam war march

WILPF SA Annual Reports, 1970

The reports record the following:

The year 1970 was a most challenging year for SA WILPF women. This challenge arose from the Moratorium demonstrations in May and September, when, for the first time, we saw the peace movement acting on a national scale in ways which we were not always able to support unanimously.

The May Moratorium was held on Saturday, 9 May. About 8,000 people marched and it was generally regarded as a great success. The September Moratorium took place on Friday 18, with a general slogan of *Stop the Country to Stop the War* and with its organisers convinced that protests should be in the form of a real challenge to authority in order to be effective. A hostile press and the withdrawal of support from the ALP contributed to a very tense atmosphere in Adelaide of the day of the march. In spite of this, about 6,000 people assembled in Elder Park and marched as far as the King William Street and North Terrace intersection where we halted. We were subsequently dispersed by the police, and 140 arrests were made.

Our WILPF branch took part in both demonstrations, marching under our WILPF banner. None of those arrested were members of WILPF. At a meeting on September 8, it was decided that we would, as a group, co-operate with the police, any refusal to obey police instructions to be a matter of individual conscience.

As a result of the September Moratorium, it has become clear that within the peace movement generally there are divided attitudes about how far protests should challenge authority, the meaning of the non-violence clause, and the extent to which opposition to American imperialism should be a factor in anti-war protests. Our WILPF branch has yet to evolve its attitudes towards these questions.

We took part in the preparations for both Moratorium demonstrations by helping with letter-boxing and other leaflet distribution, selling badges, and in the week-long 'occupation of a public place' which preceded both demonstrations.

Before the May Moratorium we decided to have shopping bags printed with Moratorium and anti-war slogans on them, and hand them out at shopping centres. It proved difficult to have the shopping bags made but we were able to buy shopping bags with string handles and to have labels printed. We prepared the shopping bags and handed them out in a successful morning at the Adelaide Central Market.

In May, we had an advertisement printed in *The Advertiser* inviting women to march with us, which resulted in new members and more women marching. We contributed money towards an advertisement at the same time in *The Australian* newspaper to which other WILPF branches also contributed.

Before the September Moratorium, we repeated our shopping bag demonstration at the Adelaide Show Grounds and the Adelaide Central Market on Friday, 4 September.

The 140 arrests on September 18 involved legal and other costs to which we decided to contribute 50 of our Peace Song records and proceeds from a lunch on 25 November at which Lynn Arnold, Chairman of the Vietnam Moratorium Committee, was our speaker. We gave $50 to the fund, coming from proceeds from this lunch. It also resulted in a donation of $100 which was distributed in our name.

In July, the *Peace Pledge Union* organised a weekend seminar on Indo-China and we helped by providing and serving the lunch on the Sunday.

In November, we were asked by WILPF National Executive to assist Victoria in publication of a leaflet relating the National Service Act to the Declaration of Human Rights. We did this and the leaflet, published in SA, was ready for all WILPF branches to use on Human Rights Day, 10 December. On this day, we staged a 9am vigil outside the AMP building, carrying placards which said, *Release John Martin* and *End the National Service Act*. In the evening, our members distributed the leaflet again at a performance of 'Out of Prison' arranged by Amnesty International.

The Milo Theatre Company offered to put on their 'Palace of Varieties' as a fundraiser for us which raised $100.

WILPF SA Branch records, 1971

The reports record the following. In January 1971, WILPF planned a weekend seminar on *Social Order and the Right to Dissent* sponsored by the Department of Adult Education in November. We were asked to provide a chairperson for the session on *Industrial Protest: The Right to Strike* which was ably done by Molly Brannigan.

Speakers at WILPF monthly meetings included Professor Duncan on *Laos*, Dr Peter Burns on *Malaysia 1968*, Professor Browning on *Population and Pollution*, Lynn Arnold on *The Future of Protest*, and Mr E. le Seur *Problems of Aborigines in our cities*.

During 1970 and again in 1971, we committed to provide the WILPF Australia National Executive. These four offices have been filled by President Marjorie Ladkin, Vice President Maud McBriar, Secretary Margaret Forte and Edna Hutchesson, Treasurer.

WILPF members were asked to send Christmas cards to Australian prisoners of conscience, which we did.

Again, WILPF woman, Margaret Forte was elected to the *Vietnam Moratorium Committee*, which is described in WILPF Minutes as 'a broadly based group, including academics, trade union representatives, representatives of women's groups and a representative of the Australian Labor Party. The Committee planned a variety of protests around the week beginning on Monday, 4 May and culminating on Saturday, 9 May.

WILPF women again had shopping bags with slogans and balloons with messages organised for distribution at peace events.

At WILPF SA's September 1971 meeting, the Minutes record that:

> As a result of their *John Zarb (Conscientious Objector)* protest 1,865 signatures had been collected and that the Petition for his release had been presented in the House of Representatives on August 12 by Mr Clyde Cameron MHR. This, together with a women-only march carrying *Release John Zarb* banners through the city on August 2, and a day-long vigil outside the AMP Building was their best organised protest this year.[10]

WILPF women followed this up the following week with a 9am to 5pm silent vigil of two women standing, one on each side of the King

William Street, entrance to the AMP building, each holding a 'Release Zarb' placard. Sixteen women took part in relays. WILPF women collected signatures for their *Free John Zarb Petition*. He was released from Pentridge Gaol (Melbourne) in August 1969 as the United States began to withdraw their troops and Australian troops began pulling out of Vietnam in 1970.

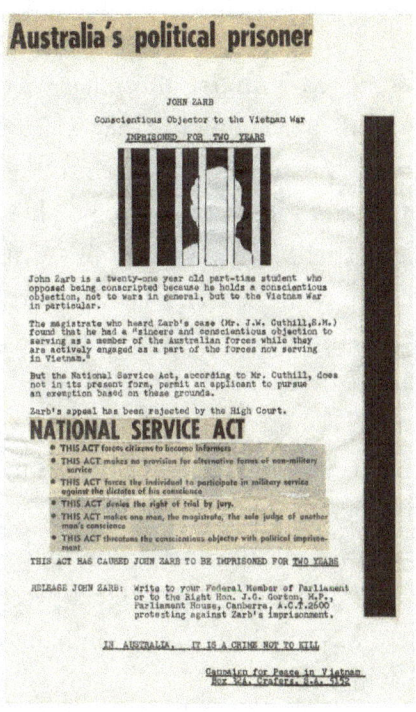

Australia's Political Prisoner: John Zarb
State Library of SA

A new project was organised by Mrs Janet Darling named *Australian Committee of Responsibility for the Children of Vietnam*. This Committee planned to help the children in practical ways, based on advice from teams of Quakers working among them in Vietnam. Janet would report on the work from time to time and donations from all were welcomed.

Janet was active in both WILPF and another organisation *Save Our Sons*. She spent years fundraising in all sorts of ways, holding regular garden parties at her home. Her focus was on supporting Vietnamese orphanages after the war ended. She received an OAM for her work.

After the Vietnam war ended, Dr Bev Hall was in the first Western delegation to visit Vietnam. They looked at the devastation and what was needed to be done to assist the Vietnamese villagers to rebuild. Bev's attention was on the Vietnamese women. She voluntarily went to help the devastated village women to set up early childhood programmes.

Bev was also associated with *The Australian/Vietnam Society* which worked together with the trade unions. They wanted to show the local people that not every Australian was against them. They organised projects such as the rebuilding of the Xuyemoc hospital as a goodwill gesture where there had been a massacre by Australian troops. She worked in collaboration with the local people and responded according to their needs. Bev was involved with establishing early childhood programmes adapted to their culture. She regularly visited Vietnam and it became at the heart of her life for several years.

At their November 1971 meeting, WILPF women redefined their WILPF Goals and programme in preparation for a new leaflet to be printed. They also agreed WILPF contribute funds and put our name to a joint peace organisation which paid for a peace advertisement in the newspaper. There was a visit to SA of Vietnamese Buddhist monk, Thich Nhat Hanh which many WILPF members attended and later published three of his poems. An ALP leaflet on their position on the Vietnam war was distributed.

On *Human Rights Day*, 11 December, a special ceremony was held in the Teacher's Training College Theatre.

Across 1971, WILPF SA actions included:

- Published Dr Tregenza's speech on conscription;
- Organised a march when Prime Minister Mr Holt was in Adelaide for the Festival of Arts;
- Sponsored three performances of Anthony Robert's readings of protest poetry;

- Planned study groups about Vietnam, Conscription and Aboriginal welfare;
- Invited Alan Ward, Fred Whitney and Elizabeth Allen to speak on each of our study group topics;
- Arranged a lunch hour meeting for Professor Manning Clark;
- Arranged two successful meetings for Joyce Mercy, which brought us in touch with SA Aborigines; and
- Arranged an evening meeting where Catherine Ellis spoke to about 60 people on Aboriginal music.

IN VIETNAM

"The latest battles make it clear that what Vietnamisation has done is to build up huge Vietnamise armies and set them at each other's throats.

"The scope and intensity of the latest assaults confirm that the North Vietnamese military strength is still very powerful and that many more years of bloody warfare can be expected."

The Deputy Federal Opposition Leader, Mr. Barnard,
in *The Australian*, 5/4/72.

"IGLOO WHITE" IS NOT THE ANSWER

- All foreign troops, "advisers", and military equipment must be withdrawn from Indo-China.

- Peace must be worked for at the conference table.

REAL AND EFFECTIVE PEACE does not depend on strategies based on weapons of terror, but on long-term policies directed towards making peace a reality.

The W.I.L.P.F. believes such policies should include—

- promoting comprehensive disarmament,

- strengthening the U.N. and supporting and extending its machinery for pre-conflict reconciliation,

- recognition of the right to national self-determination by all countries, and of their right to change their social and political systems without fear of interference from outside states,

- Economic aid to the developing countries, especially through generous trade and tariff agreements, and stabilised prices for the commodities on which their economies depend.

1972 IS ELECTION YEAR. DISCUSS FOREIGN POLICY WITH THE CANDIDATES IN YOUR ELECTORATE. THE FUTURE OF YOUR CHILDREN DEPENDS UPON A SANE FOREIGN POLICY.

SA branch flyer 'Igloo White,' opposing laser-guided bombing

SA WILPF woman Cynthia James' speech on why she opposed the Vietnam war.

Cynthia James remained an active member of WILPF until she died in 2022. In 1988, she explained to students at Adelaide High School why she opposed the Vietnam War and why she was a peace activist. Cynthia was born in Mildura in 1922 and educated in Melbourne, obtaining her M.SC in 1946. She was employed as a Research Officer working on plant alkaloids in the CSIRO.

She married mathematician Alan James in 1950. They moved to the United States and had four children. She worked as a Research Assistant at the Botany Department, Colombia University New York. Aware of early warning signs of the United States of America government's likely war in Vietnam, her family returned to live in Australia, settling in Adelaide.

The following are excerpts from her 1988 speech given on Anzac Day:

As I prepared this talk, I thought a good deal about my own High School years. I went to a small all-girls school and had on the whole a rather sheltered upbringing. This was during the 1930s and WW1 was still very much in people's minds and conversations. Anzac Day was real and immediate, and taken very seriously.

When I was ten, Hitler came to power in Germany. During my teenage years, war clouds gathered over Europe and overshadowed all my development. Despite the efforts of the League of Nations, tension grew in Europe and on September 3, 1939, Britain and France declared war on Germany and Australia followed suit straight away.

I had no idea what war meant to peoples' personal lives, how horrifying, how overpowering, how all-embracing it must inevitably become. I spent the war years as a Science student at Melbourne University and did the 'little bits expected of me' – knitted countless socks, netted camouflage nets between lectures, summer jobs at munitions factories, helped dig trenches in the University grounds. With so many men away at war the university probably had the highest proportion of women students it ever had – my final physiology class had thirteen women and one man.

By the final years of the war, I had come to a few tentative conclusions:

First, I could never enter the armed forces. I could never take the sort of mindless discipline required nor entertain the idea of being part of the military machine.

Second, I was sad beyond measure about the sacrifice of the young people, civilians, old people, towns, buildings and countryside which happened in Europe and Asia on both sides of the armed forces, and I was horrified by the atomic bombing of Japan.

The 1950s and 1960s were a period of blossoming and growth and liberation for everyone. There were consumer goods that we had never seen in our lives – remember that the 1930s were depression years and the 1940s were war years – overseas travel became possible and the whole world seemed to suddenly open up. The United Nations was formed, and we all thought the world would achieve some sort of peaceful existence.

Anzac Day became quite meaningless, even abhorrent to me. I thought to myself, why do we still celebrate a military blunder, the loss of human life, the hatred of the Turks, the futility of war, and think that this is what made Australia and New Zealand into nations.

But again, international relations deteriorated and in the 1960s, America became involved in the Vietnam war. I was very much against this involvement and took the step of joining one of the peace groups – the Women's International League for Peace and Freedom. My eyes were certainly opened when I read the history of the organisation. Here were women who had come together across enemy lines in 1915 and met in Holland to talk peace during the war. After WWI they formed an international organisation which is still flourishing.

They were perceptive enough to point out the injustices of the Versailles Treaty and predict the problems it would cause. They were active in shaping the League of Nations and later the United Nations and they are still active in spreading the idea of the non-violent and just solution of conflict.

I felt I had been very slow to wake up to the idea that one must look for the seeds of a conflict and seek a just solution to it. If one can find a just and equitable solution, then war becomes pointless and meaningless.

During the Vietnam war, another aspect of Anzac Day was made clear to me by the actions of a group of perspective people who, for many years, attended the dawn service on Anzac Day and other memorial services and held up peace banners there. They have shown another face of Anzac Day. They have pleaded for peace, have drawn attention to the futility of war and have alerted many people to the idea that peace is something to be sought and worked for. They have looked to the future not brooded over the past.

When I was young, the peace movement was oblivious, or not well recognised. I know there have always been those people who abhorred violence and sought peace, often at great cost to themselves. The Quakers have always had non-violence as one of their main tenets. There were many pacifists in the first World War – Bertrand Russell was probably the best known of them and I'm sure you have read some of the poetry of the WWI poets like Wilfred Own and Siegfried Sassoon. But there was not the great grass roots movement that we see now and it this worldwide desire for peace that gives us hope today.

Cynthia James was WILPF SA's longest serving member and much loved by all. She died in her late nineties, still a WILPF member.

[1] *More than a Hat and Glove Brigade, The Story of the Union of Australian Women*, pp.79-80.
[2] www.rslnsw.org.au: The Vietnam war.
[3] *More than a Hat and Glove Brigade, The Story of the Union of Australian Women*, p.80.
[4] Ibid, p.80.
[5] Australian War Memorial website.
[6] Conscription during the Vietnam war – collections.slsa.sa.gov.au
[7] Australian War Memorial website.
[8] www.rslnsw.org.au The Vietnam War.
[9] www.awm.gov.au viet_opp.
[10] Minutes of WILPF SA Meeting dated Tuesday, 16 September 1971.

5

WILPF SA Branch Peace Campaigns, 1980-2000

Introduction

During this period, the key issue facing the world remained the potential that nuclear weapons held could annihilate whole cities and countries. Disarmament was the only sensible way forward. Slowly, the concept of resolving international relations through the United Nations Security Council was taking effect with the withdrawal of Soviet troops from Afghanistan in 1989.

Then there was a UN backed peace pact in Cambodia in 1991. A UN peacekeeping force was sent to Croatia, then handed over to NATO missions in 1994 with the *Washington Agreement* brokered between the Republic of Bosnia and Herzegovina and the Croatian Republic of Herzeg-Bosnia. Successful negotiations to end the eight-year war between Iran and Iraq were reached in 1998. It was hoped that this new international agency would be able to solve differences between countries and negotiate peaceful settlements.

Despite these encouraging signs of brokering peace, what soon developed was an arms race. Australia saw advantages in selling weapons through promotion by government *Arms Fairs* and increasing their military capacity through the acquisition of military hardware'.[1] This is a direction that WILPF opposes.

WILPF SA Works with Other Peace Groups

WILPF SA's branch cooperation with other peace groups increased over these decades, especially with the *United Nations Association*, with a WILPF representative on their Executive. WILPF also worked with the *UN Association of Australia Disarmament Committee*, the *Campaign for an Independent East Timor*, the *Peace Information Exchange*, the *Status of Women Committee, Time for Peace, Australian Anti-Bases Campaign Coalition*, the *Australian Peace Committee* and various church groups.

WILPF SA women's contribution to the 1980 federal election was to publish an open letter to the Prime Minister calling for an independent Australian foreign policy. They followed this up the following year with a questionnaire to all SA Members of the House of Representatives regarding foreign bases in Australia.

In 1981, WILPF held a successful, well attended seminar on *Peace and the Nuclear Threat* with Senator Ruth Coleman as the key-note speaker. WILPF women also attended and contributed to the Alice Springs Easter Conference Seminar on *Foreign Bases*.

Tensions were still high worldwide over potential nuclear threats. When the anti-nuclear film *The Day After* was screened at the Academy Theatre in 1982, WILPF members handed out specially prepared leaflets on ways that individuals could express opposition to the nuclear threat.

In the years 1982, 1983 and 1984, WILPF arranged winter lunch programmes with invited speakers on the topics *Our Near Neighbours, Alternative Future Policies for Australia* and *What can anyone Do about the Arms Race?* There were three meetings in each series which drew good audiences.

International Peace Day booklet, 1983

In 1983, WILPF women attended the protest camp at Roxby Downs. One of our members was among those arrested for 'loitering' and was surprised about media reports of 'violence' as she considered it had been a peaceful protest.

The following year, they joined other groups for a protest camp at Pine Gap, and associated protests at Salisbury Weapons Research Centre and Nurrungar.

WILPF organised a 1984 June meeting with our *Australian Ambassador for Disarmament*, Richard Butler. They had 30 people attending, representing 16 organisations including WILPF in the afternoon, and then later that evening, a public meeting was held with 300 attending – it was lively and controversial!

WILPF woman Janet Darling, represented WILPF at a seminar on *Major Issues in Nuclear Energy* run by the Australian Mineral Foundation. She then spent two days at the *Women's Peace Camp* set up outside the Defence Research Centre at Salisbury, an outer, northern suburb of Adelaide.

The year 1985 was a busy year for WILPF. The topic for their February meeting was *MX Missiles and the significance of the ANZUS Treaty*. This followed a decision by the Australian Government to assist with the US testing of MX missiles off the Australian coast. Janet Darling wrote to the Secretary of the SA Australian Labor Party protesting the decision and the way in which it was reached. She and others also wrote to all SA Members of the House of Representatives and the Senate regarding the testing of MX missiles in Australian waters and asking their views on nuclear issues. They were pleased to receive a good response to their letters.

WILPF women began collecting signatures for the International WILPF petition for a *Total Nuclear Test Ban*. This petition was presented to the UN General Assembly in 1986, the *International Year for Peace*. Two SA peace activists were awarded Commonwealth peace medals – Eric Bogle for his peace songs such as, *And the band played Waltzing Matilda*, and Jim Gale for many years of peace activism.

In March 1985, WILPF women attended the annual Palm Sunday rally along with other peace organisations and church groups.

In June 1985, the *Australian Pacific Women's Conference* was held in Sydney with 300 women attending, including 30 women from the Pacific Islands and Pacific Rim countries. This conference was a prelude to the Nairobi Conference to mark the end of the *UN Decade for Women*. It was one of the largest and most successful conferences organised by WILPF in Australia. Four women from the SA branch attended.

WILPF woman Molly Brannigan was then sponsored by the South Australian government to attend the Nairobi Conference in July and report back to the local women's groups and the SA Government.

Once again, WILPF women interested schools in participating in their *Junior Media Peace Project* (JUMP), an art and music peace project which began in 1983. The aim was to invite young people to write, draw or otherwise express 'ideas for a better world'. This project involved liaison with schools throughout the year and an exhibition was opened on UN Day, 24 October. School children designed and entered peace posters each year for a prize. It was a very engaging project taken up by many Adelaide primary schools. It ran for ten years, promoting peace in schools and was organised by Margaret Forte, Cynthia James and the SA Branch.

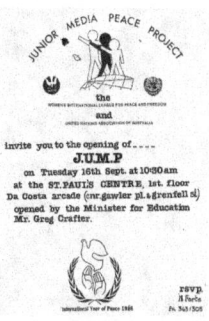

Junior Media Peace Project

WILPF women then prepared material for the *Decade of Women Exhibition* held at the Old Legislative Council Library in the Constitutional Museum.

Next, the women held a candlelight procession to commemorate *Hiroshima Week* and had a stall at the Human Rights Day *Fair-Go Fair* held in Elder Park. There were always plenty of WILPF tea towels and badges to buy as well as lots of leaflets on current issues, thanks to Cynthia James who managed all the WILPF merchandise. The key aim was to make local people aware of each issue, the consequences and an action they could take to address that situation.

In 1986, to celebrate the *UN International Year of Peace*, SA WILPF women organised another school children's peace art and music project with the same name as last year - *Junior Media Peace Project* (JUMP). It was displayed in St Paul's Centre for four weeks and opened by the Minister of Education, Lynn Arnold.

Two WILPF members, Margaret Forte and Stewart Barnes, received the Medal of the Order of Australia (OAM) for their service to peace. Margaret's work had been for her WILPF work over many years. Stewart Barnes had coordinated the Junior Media Peace Project in SA as well as being the honorary secretary of the UNAA (SA) Division for some years.

Margaret Forte receives an OAM award, here with Cynthia James and Maude McBriar

WILPF *Twin Cities Project* was innovative. WILPF and the Union of Australian Women received a state grant of $1000 to mount a display in the Speakers Corner in Old Parliament House for February 1987. The exhibition of sixteen panels was developed by groups in Adelaide, showcasing both St Louis in the State of Missouri, USA, and Minsk in Byelo province, Russia, USSR. The aim was to bring potentially antagonistic nations closer together through recognising their common humanity, by working together on this project, and sharing their desire for peaceful relations between their two countries. Sadly, no enduring relationships occurred.

The State Government funded an *Adult Peace Education Officer*, Mr David Trebilcock, who was supported by 17 organisations of which WILPF was one. WILPF also assisted five local libraries in establishing peace resource centres.

WILPF participated with a stall at the *Palm Sunday March* and the *Peace Fair* in Rymill Park. Fairs were always a happy way to meet and greet lots of friends as well as engage others who may not be aware of some of our current campaigns for peace.

Invited speakers for WILPF monthly meetings that year were Dr Bev Hall, who had recently returned from a working tour of Nicaragua, Vietnam and Kampuchea; David Trebilcock from the Adelaide Peace Education Office, Don Aspinall who spoke on Indonesia and Kathy Bodnar told us about the *Teachers for Peace program*.

A large part of WILPF's work was to educate people on the current issues facing Australians.

WILPF Activities

1988 to 1989

The Bicentennial 1988, marked the 200th anniversary of the arrival of the First Fleet of British Convict ships at Sydney, 1788. WILPF acknowledges the colonisation of this land.

The *Royal Commission into Black Deaths in Custody* was established to 'study and report upon the underlying social, cultural and legal issues behind the deaths in custody of Aboriginal people and Torres Strait Islanders, in the light of the high level of such deaths.' When the Commission met in Adelaide, several WILPF members attended sessions and reported back. The full report was not released until 1991. One of the outcomes was the establishment of a *National Deaths in Custody Monitoring and Research Programme* at the Australian Institute of Criminology.[2]

WILPF women supported Aboriginal woman, Ruby Hammond in her campaign to enter State Parliament, but she was unsuccessful. For their Bicentennial project, WILPF SA chose to write to businesses urging them to employ Aboriginal staff and received some encouraging replies. They enjoyed participating in the annual Palm Sunday march and the stall in Peace Park afterwards and then later, the more sombre Hiroshima Day rally.

WILPF worked with the *Australian Peace Committee, UNAA, Anti Bases Campaign Coalition*, the *Status of Women Committee*, the *East Timor Committee*, the *Council of Churches Stop the Killing in Mozambique* campaign, as well as the organisation, *Time for Peace*, which was campaigning against violent toys.

WILPF held two public meetings during 1989. The first was in April with speaker Bill Guy, Foreign Editor of *The Advertiser* speaking on Indonesia, with the topic *Getting along with our neighbours* and in September, Foundation Professor of East Asian Studies, Prof. Gavan McCormack spoke on *Japan*.

In July 1989, WILPF's 24th International Triennial Congress was held in Sydney with the theme *Women Building a Common and Secure Future*. WILPF SA branch agreed to take on *WILPF Australian Section Secretariat*. The Congress met on the eve of WILPF's 75th Anniversary. This was the first time it had been held in the Southern hemisphere! WILPF Aboriginal member, Kay Mundine, gave the opening address. The Congress was opened by Eleonore Romberg, WILPF International President, with WILPF member and Australian Senator, Margaret Reynolds (Qld) giving a keynote speech. Later, Australian Aboriginal woman leader, Barbara Shaw (from Alice Springs), also addressed the Congress, outlining the key issues of discrimination for Aboriginal people. She finished her speech with these words:

> We will continue to struggle to survive, to search for answers, solutions, strategies to deal with the injustice, violence, poverty, deprivation and senseless sufferings that we know of, and for which purpose we have come together to share our insights, experiences and hopes: to build a common and secure future with you.[3]

In the WILPF Australian Section Report to Congress, they stated that Australian branches had taken action on war victims and war toys, food irradiation, domestic violence, conversion, Brundtland report,

WOMEN'S INTERNATIONAL LEAGUE FOR PEACE AND FREEDOM

refugee and humanitarian migrant intake, needs of Pacific Island women who are resident in Australia and permanent residence for West Papua refugees.[4]

Six women went from SA branch to the *WILPF International Congress* (Maud McBriar, Coralie Nichols, Margaret Forte, Cynthia James, Janet Darling and Stewart Barnes), attending different workshops on Environment, Conflict Resolution, Economic Questions, Indigenous Peoples, and Disarmament. There were representatives present from Australia, Bolivia, Chile, Costa Rica, Denmark, Federal Republic of Germany, Finland, France, Israel, Italy, Japan, Mauritius, The Netherlands, New Zealand, Norway, Palestine, Sri Lanka, Sweden, Switzerland and the United States of America. It was exhilarating to be part of such an international gathering of WILPF peace women!

WILPF Australian Section President wrote to Senators about their concerns with Australia's developing arms trade.

In SA, the 25 November state election was held. Prior to this, women sent all candidates seven questions regarding protection of the environment, uranium mining, establishment of a multi-function polis, peace education, military equipment, Freedom of Information Act, and Aboriginal welfare. They received 17 replies so thought this was a valuable exercise. The same year, WILPF women attended the Alice Springs Easter Conference concerning foreign bases.

WILPF, along with other peace groups, began protests at Port Adelaide during visits from possibly nuclear-powered or armed ships.

The WILPF branch has supported and at times helped to organise marches for such occasions as *Palm Sunday* and *Hiroshima Day* and with functions arranged for *United Nations Day* on 24 October and *Human Rights Day* on 10 December.

Because WILPF is a small group, it has been grateful for opportunities to work with other groups with similar aims. When there are areas of difference, we work out a *friendly compromise*. The aims of WILPF were first set down at the inaugural International Congress in 1919 and have remained unaltered. A condition of membership is a willingness to accept these aims, the first of which states:

WILPF aims at bringing together women of different political and philosophical tendencies united in their determination to study, make known and help abolish the political, social, economic and psychological causes of war, and to work constructively for peace.

The women looked forward to another productive year spreading the word for peaceful resolution of conflict.

Women in Black monthly vigils were held on Parliament House steps for eight years. The SA branch campaign *Keep Space for Peace* continued for ten years.

The AIDEX Arms Fair Exhibition, Canberra, 1991

For some years, the peace movement had been aware of the Australian government's manufacture and sale of arms to various warring nations such as Pakistan and Saudi Arabia. The Australian Government promoted sales worldwide by holding annual Arms Fairs – named AIDEX.

At the AIDEX 1991 exhibition in Canberra, many protest groups, trade unions and individuals held peaceful demonstrations. They had organised together beforehand through a collective - *STOP AIDEX Campaign*. The organisers had arranged camping, water, toilets and all facilities, as well as working with the police to ensure the march on the Saturday would be peaceful. There were around 1,000 people using the allocated campsite, with many others staying with friends.

The main event was to be a protest march (estimated 3,000) with pickets beforehand to stop weapons entering the exhibition hall. The Secretary of the Trades and Labour Council participated officially. A picket line was set up to ask drivers delivering weapons for exhibition, to not proceed with their delivery. Some did turn around as they supported the goals of the protest. The Quakers had applied for a stall at the Arms Trade Fair but were refused.

WILPF Demonstration with balloons - Janice High, Miriam Tonkin, Cathy Picone

Charmaine Greiger on the WILPF stall

WILPF women from all states and several from SA, made their own placards with messages such as *The Arms Trade misuses the earth's resources* and *The Arms trade diverts wealth away from the needs of the people*. The women holding them reported that those reading them seemed to be affected by their message. This huge protest was getting a lot of media attention Australia wide, thus informing people of the government's trade deals in arms, and citizens' opposition to weapons sales.

The day before the exhibition opened, the police moved in to make mass arrests, so protestors blocked the road further down. It became a violent melee over the next few days with many police arrests and violence. This continued for the rest of the week. It was the worst Australian conflict between peace protestors and the government. A full account (500 pages) was produced by *Friends of the Hearings 1991-1995*.

Sadly, these trade arms fairs continue today. Each year since, in South Australia, a group of dedicated peace activists have protested peacefully at the entrance to the Conference Centre on North Terrace. You may care to join us!

1991 to 2000

WILPF promoted the second edition of Keith Suter's book *Changes needed for a New World Order*.

They continued to have excellent guest speakers at their meetings:

- Michael Sullivan, Lecturer in International Relations, Politics Department of Flinders University, gave a talk on *The Middle East – its background and its future;*
- Silver Moon spoke on *Greenham Common's place in the 1992 peace movement;*
- *A world without weapons* seminar was held; and
- A talk was given by Ed Irons who represented the UNAA at the ASPAC 1990 'Conference for Disarmament Security and Cooperation in the Pacific' on *Facing problems in the Pacific.*

These are just some examples of the wide range of issues that women were keen to learn about.

WILPF women attended a national conference on the *Campaign Against Racial Exploitation* (CARE).

Women were also becoming aware of the destruction of our environment and the *Greenhouse effect*. Tasmanian WILPF branch wrote about French nuclear tests on Kerguelen Islands in the Pacific resulting in fallout over Tasmania. WILPF International was collecting signatures for a petition to support the *Comprehensive Test Ban Treaty*.

In 1992, WILPF held a big exhibition *A New World Order – for Whom?* at Old Parliament House.

Annual Palm Sunday rallies for peace in Adelaide: Senator Rosemary Crowley, longtime WILPF member receiving rainbow petition to support Aboriginal rights, 1992.

In 1993, WILPF women's response to reconciliation was to organise a *Through Aboriginal Eyes* exhibition for the International Year of the World's Indigenous Peoples.

In 1994, WILPF SA hosted the Australian Section meeting in Adelaide and took over the running of our national office again with a grant from the Office of the Status of Women for rent and administration.

WILPF Australian Section Office, 155 Pirie Street, Adelaide, Janice High and Leonie Ebert, 1990

SA International Women's Day, 1994

WILPF Information stall in the Adelaide parklands: Jill Bundy, Jilinda Thompson, Cynthia James, Cathy Picone, Heather Crosby, 1995

WILPF's 80th anniversary and 26th *International Congress* occurred in 1995 and was held in Helsinki, in September. A *Peace Train* was organised for women to travel from Helsinki to Beijing, China. This was the first time this route had been traversed by a train. It was to be a similar 'crossing of the borders' that their foremothers did to attend their historic 1915 Conference. On the twenty-two-day journey, the Peace Train participants took part in a range of activities and workshops on the train relating to peace, development, equality and lifestyle. 223 women and 9 men came from all walks of life, from 40 countries, ranging in age from 18 to 86.

WILPF Peace Train to Beijing, 1995

Three SA WILPF women participated in this historic journey, Léonie Ebert Smith, her daughter Naomi and sister-in-law Gil Smith. They met women of Kyiv and discussed the Chernobyl nuclear disaster. Reflecting on her memories, Léonie recalls being told that, 'There is not a square inch of uncontaminated soil in the country.' This beautiful city is experiencing disaster and heartbreak again. In personal reflections of the 1995 Peace Train, written in 2022, she writes, 'I feel an unbearable sadness for the women of Ukraine and their country. And now Ukraine is also being threatened with the use of nuclear weapons.'

These women talked also with physicians and leaders of women's organisations in Kazakhstan who described their struggle against Russian nuclear testing. They asked those of us who were attending the World Conference on Women in Beijing to take a message to Beijing *'halt all nuclear testing.'*

Since then, Léonie has joined the *International Campaign to Abolish Nuclear Weapons* (ICAN), the *Women's Climate Congress* (WCC), and devotes herself to *The Graham F Smith Peace Foundation* which works for peace through the arts. In a summary to WILPF SA, *Linking Some Peace Train Memories with Life Today*, she explains that:

> The Peace Foundation widens its scope by acknowledging and connecting with likeminded organisations such as WILPF, ICAN, WCC and The Independent and Peaceful Australia Network (IPAN) which is a network of organisations around Australia – community, faith and peace groups, trade unions and concerned individuals – aiming to build public dialogue and pressure for change to a truly independent foreign policy for Australia – one in which our government plays a positive role in solving international conflicts peacefully.

In Beijing, women attended the *UN Fourth World Conference on Women*, which went for nine days from 30th August - 8th September 1995. This proved to be the most progressive conference for women's agenda for peace ever held. 17,000 women from all over the world participated, representing 189 governments.

UN Fourth World Conference on Women, 1995

They developed the *Beijing Platform for Action* with the aim of gender equality and empowerment of women everywhere. The twelve areas of concern they identified for action are -

1. Women and the environment
2. Women and poverty
3. The girl child (genital mutilation)
4. Education and training
5. Women and health
6. Violence against women
7. Women and armed conflict
8. Women and the economy
9. Women in power and decision making
10. Institutional mechanisms
11. Human rights of women
12. Women and the media.

This is still a progressive agenda for women today, but sadly it has not been fully implemented due to conservative forces blocking progress whenever it comes up for debate in the United Nations.

WILPF Australian Section Conference in Adelaide, Stewart Barnes and Cynthia James (SA) and Mary Ziesak (Qld), 1997

Yumi (SA) with Dr
Margot Roe (Tas), 1997

In 1998, WILPF organised three workshops on *Human Rights*. On 26 October, Cathy Picone, WILPF Australian Section National Coordinator and SA Coordinator, wrote on behalf of WILPF Australia to Foreign Minister Alexander Downer to urge him to support the *New Agenda Coalition* by Ireland, South Africa, Brazil, Egypt, Slovakia, New Zealand, Sweden and Mexico to support their nuclear disarmament initiative, but sadly Mr Downer declined.[5]

Two workshops were held on *Women in Armed Conflict* in 1999.

In 2000, WILPF women all over the world, especially in Australia and SA, celebrated the *World March of Women 2000*.

Over time, new women always seemed to become involved with WILPF and spend several years actively engaged with the peace issues of their time. It is a challenging but enjoyable occupation with a sense of satisfaction that we are doing something to make peace an issue and hopefully a reality for all.

[1] 'Piecing it Together – hearing the stories of AIDEX 91 – a report prepared by Friends of the Hearings 1991-1995, pp18-19.

[2] www.en.m.wikipedia.org Royal Commission on Deaths in Custody report.

[3] Speech notes of Aboriginal woman Barbara Shaw, published *in*

'Report of the 24th Congress of WILPF 'Women Building A Common and Secure Future' – Sydney, Australia 14-25 July 1989, p.9.

[4] Australian Section Report to 24th Congress of WILPF – Sydney 1989, p.57.

[5] WILPF letter to Foreign Minister, Alexander Downer dated 26 October, 1998 – WILPF SA archives.

6

The Illegal US War on Iraq, 2003

Events Leading Up to the Illegal US Invasion of Iraq

Prior to 2002, the UN Security Council had passed 16 resolutions on Iraq. In 2002, the Security Council unanimously passed Resolution 1441 offering Iraq under Saddam Hussein 'a final opportunity to comply with its disarmament obligations that had been set out in several previous resolutions (Resolutions 660, 661, 678, 686, 687, 707, 715, 986 and 1284).' The US said this provided justification for what was subsequently termed the 'US invasion of Iraq.'[1]

A year later, in March 2003, the United States Government announced that 'diplomacy has failed' and that it would proceed with a 'coalition of the willing' to rid Iraq under Saddam Hussein of weapons of mass destruction the US insisted it possessed. The 2003 invasion of Iraq began a few days later.[2]

On 16 September 2004, then Secretary-General of the United Nations, Kofi Annan, speaking on the invasion, said, 'I have indicated it was not in conformity with the UN Charter. From our point of view, from the Charter point of view, it was illegal.'[3]

The Australian legal profession said any pre-emptive invasion was illegal; the churches said it would be a humanitarian disaster; the Returned Soldiers League said war traumatises all those involved; the Senate Parliamentarians voted against any involvement; but our Constitution does not compel a Prime Minister to get a vote through parliament to commit troops overseas. Then Prime Minister John Howard loudly proclaimed that 'I alone will make the decision' and that 'I have not made my mind up yet' even though troops had sailed in readiness for invasion.

All over Australia, opposition to war was mounting daily. Adelaideans were not alone in opposing war. Huge rallies occurred around the world. In SA, the *Australian Peace Committee* called a meeting of various peace groups to set up an effective *No War* committee. No War organised many anti-war rallies and mounted the biggest anti-war march in SA's history - marchers were still at Victoria Square with thousands crammed all the way to Parliament House on Saturday, 16 February 2003. It is claimed that 100,000 people attended.

'Today We Own the Streets: Adelaide No War Rally of 16 September 2003'

Courtesy of David Faber, Labour History Melbourne

Ruth Russell was the WILPF speaker at this SA march, and their representative on the No War committee. It was a truly inspiring event. Her short speech gave her reasons for going to Iraq.

> This is a defining moment in Australia's history. Now is the moment when we must decide whether we want to behave like a civilised society.
>
> I remember the euphoria and elation all Australians felt at the opening of the Olympic Games in Sydney. How we welcomed people from all nations. That same year at the beginning of the new millennium, the United Nations set out a Declaration and Programme of Action for a culture of peace. The Declaration stated: 'Peace is always possible and violence avoidable.' John Howard said his government was

not interested in supporting this international year for the culture of peace.

Now only two years later, Australia has changed from a culture of trust and understanding to a culture of fear, repression, intolerance and now ultimate violence – WAR.

We cannot let John Howard and his government destroy our unique Australian way of life and society. Keep on speaking out - *We must oppose war and build peace.*

Peace Activists in Iraq

This chapter tells some of Ruth Russell's story. Ruth had a hectic time as soon as she arrived in Baghdad, where there were more than 500 people registering as 'human shields' from over 20 countries. A few hours after she arrived, she learnt that SA's Channel Seven had sent a TV crew to cover her arrival. This was great because that afternoon there was to be a huge 'human shield march' through the main streets of Baghdad with each group walking under their country's banner. Someone was to organise all the banners.

When Ruth went to collect her Australian banner, she found it was spelt 'Austria'. Knowing Channel 7 TV crew would be filming, Ruth and Donna Mulhearn from NSW, Ruth rushed to get more paper, coloured writing pens and quickly made a new 'Australia' banner. Everyone marched in style, proudly carrying their national banners and were enthralled to receive a wondrous welcome from the local Iraqi people. We were surrounded by international TV crews.

When we got to a famous Iraqi statue, blonde Donna hugged a little black-haired Iraqi girl of four who made the peace sign. Their photo went round the world! It was an extraordinary event to have the world's media, local Iraqis and people from so many nationalities united for peace! Two days before the war started, 20 South Africans arrived with a blessing from Nelson Mandela. It was a truly international movement. In all, ten Australians joined as human shields.

The United Nations had a huge office in Baghdad, so human shields organised to work under their guidance. The UN told us which 'civilian humanitarian sites' we could protect by going and living on the premises. The aim was to let the US know that humanitarian sites were being protected and should not be bombed, should war eventuate. Ruth chose to protect the Taji Food silo which stored all the Australian wheat, most of which was from Coonalpyn, the Site Manager told Ruth when he heard she was from South Australia.

Every evening there were passionate meetings with each group translating details into their own language. Meetings often lasted until midnight. Ruth helped to manage the Media Centre with Donna Mulhearn, an accomplished Australian journalist. A *Human Shield Register* was set up so there was a record of everyone in case of war. Everyone could choose which site we would 'protect' and send personal messages to our countryfolk to let them know what was happening. The US said they would jail any American who stayed on as a human shield, so many were urged to return before the war started. It is salient to reflect that America, which prides itself as 'the land of the free' would imprison peace activists for seven years if they remained in Iraq once war started!

During the two weeks before the war started, everyone was invited to many Iraqi cultural events – one was *International Women's Day* in which we joined Iraqi women calling for peace – many dressed in their black abayas. We attended an Iraqi cultural event showcasing the best of Iraqi ballet, music and singing and the second half of the concert was for human shields to perform. Ruth chose to sing *We shall overcome* with a British folk singer and his guitar. She was asked by some local Iraqi women to follow them and was taken to a women's prayer room and had henna painted on both hands. It was so moving to be together, all understanding how precious life is and how imminent war was!

Groups visited earlier war sites which were still totally destroyed and full of depleted uranium. Ruth went to Babylon and spoke to a crowd of a few thousand local Iraqis, to let them know that activists had come from many different countries to speak out for peace. Afterwards, a little boy coyly approached her with a bag of popcorn. Then us activists were given a tour of the ancient site of Babylon, where Alexander the Great set up his last palace on the banks of the Tigris River and made the first bitumen for chariot races at the front of his palace. German archaeologists had spent years restoring some of this site.

Some human shields asked to be stationed on archaeological sites, but the Iraqi government declined, as it was more important to protect sites where civilians were living. We accepted that. After the war, we learned that the US trashed this international heritage site when they drove their tanks through after they took control.

Ruth also visited the Children's Hospital where so many young babies and children were dying of cancer as the US had blockaded medicines that would heal them. It is important that people know of the disrespect the American administration shows to other civilisations that do not comply with US demands.

The Spanish human shield group of 30 people, wanted to protect hospitals, but the Iraqis said they would be in the way with many casualties coming in. There were many things to get organised.

On 1 March 2003, an international press conference was organised to formally tell the world that human shields would be stationed at five UN designated humanitarian sites that should not be bombed – the Baghdad power station, the Taji food silo (feeding 20 million people), Jaizert Water treatment plant, the Durra Oil Refinery and the Durra Electrical power plant.

Ruth chose to move to Taji food silos with Donna, Judith (English), Annette (Scottish) and Michelle (a young woman from Perth who followed her over to Baghdad). Michelle was good at playing with the Iraqi children. Our group had been given a house that could accommodate five women - with another house for five men – 20 kms north of Baghdad, but very close to the Taji military base we found out later!

Everyone waited with bated breath for the UN Security Council meeting to debate the legality of the proposed invasion of Iraq by the

United States. It was voted 'illegal' by the Security Council, but the US and Australia said the war would start on 20 March.

We activists now had to prepare to 'stay on for whatever duration the war took'. Would it be weeks or months? No-one knew. We pooled resources but were told by the kindly Taji Wheat silo manager that we were their 'honoured guests' and they would feed us and look after us. We still had a designated car, driver, interpreter and minders who were with us wherever we went as the Iraqi government did not know if we were spies or genuine peace activists. We had to let them know where we wanted to go and when, and if it was a bona fide peace reason like visiting schools, hospitals, the press, TV stations, etc.

Donna and Ruth made several links to Australian TV networks over time – most around 5am local time so we were on the Australian evening news. We had to climb up the dark stairs to the only television studio in Baghdad on the fifth floor of a dilapidated building.

Melbourne radio announcer Derryn Hinch phoned Ruth every week to berate her for being a 'stooge for the Iraqi government.' He didn't want to know what we were really doing, only wanted to put his views across. Ruth was totally disgusted with his disingenuous approach. It makes her shudder that he late became an Australian Senator.

We still found time to visit schools, some with lovely Australian gum trees in their yards. At one school we visited, the children were asked to draw a sign to show all the international TV crews who came. Ruth still has a photo of a ten-year-old boy, holding up his sign in English *Please do not kill Iraqi children*. This is what war really is – killing indiscriminately, especially the huge bombs that the US used!

Ruth visited hospitals, organised media events and met lots of local Iraqi people who wanted to thank her for coming to stand with them. It was a very emotional time for everyone. War was due to start so she was prepared for whatever future befell her. On the first night, we heard the Allied bombers come over and learned that they were living close by the Iraqi Taji military base.

We saw numerous bombs headed that way most nights and have photos of a massive firebomb which highlighted a local Iraqi villager's clothes-line in the foreground. Ruth wanted to get out to investigate the damage, but it was forbidden. Later, back in Australia, she wanted to use these photos to mount a case in the International Court of Justice against the US Government bombing where civilians lived, but it proved difficult to proceed through all the required documentation. She still has the photos she took from her roof as irrefutable proof.

We were able to visit hospitals and talk to people there to hear their stories – all of them harrowing! Ruth has a photo of a beautiful eight-year-old girl who was lying full of shrapnel from a bomb that hit her house; they had not told her yet that all the rest of her family were dead. Although it was tough emotionally, she thought it was important to record the consequences of war on innocent civilians – they are the ones who really suffer. How dare Australians be involved in this type of behaviour!

Ruth could only get news from BBC but knew the US was closing in. Our group were barricaded in, no one could get in or out of our site. The Taji Manager told us that they expected the US to come from the north soon (they were on the northern outskirts 20 km from Baghdad centre). The day before we had our last human shield demonstration at the front of the TV broadcasting building – with Japanese, Turkish, Argentinian, Italian, Spanish and two Australians – Donna and Ruth.

On Sunday, 6 April 2003, David, an ex-US Marine who served in Vietnam and knew about war, called from the roof that he had just seen US tanks come into view on the northern highway on their way to Baghdad. Heavy artillery fire and huge explosions began. We could only sit and listen and wonder what carnage was occurring outside. We watched the Iraqi men in their compound – they met together in the centre of the street, then all went to their homes and changed into their Arab clothes – they would face the US as Arabs not westerners!

We had already thought about an escape route and what to take, everything was packed and ready if escape was required. We sewed David's precious photos inside books and Ruth sewed her films into the centre of her sleeping bag as she was determined to bring this evidence out with her. We had someone observing from our roof to let us know if invasion of our site was imminent and where to gather and execute an escape if required.

To our surprise, all the US tanks kept straight on ahead along the Northern highway into Baghdad. Lots of shelling and bombing could be heard. Later, we learnt that the US army rushed into the famous Firdir Square to topple Saddam's statue while others went to protect the Department of Oil headquarters, while still others had the signal that they could loot the amazing archaeological treasures in the Iraqi museum! Chaos and mayhem reined for three days. We heard that there were a lot of 'pay back' killings by Iraqis. It was far too dangerous to consider leaving our barricaded compound.

On Thursday, 10 April, David said he wanted to go out to film. Ruth wanted to go with him, but he slipped out at around 4am and left a message that she was to wait for his return. He returned after 7pm that night and walked in haggard and distraught. He said he couldn't speak to us now, he just had to rest as he had walked miles from the hospitals where he had seen so many civilians wounded, and walked through streets with many dead people, civilians as well as soldiers' bodies lying everywhere. It was total chaos!

The following day he recovered enough to show us some of his footage, tragic photos, evidence of horrific stories of lives destroyed and lost.

We knew then it was time to leave and get these photos out, but how and when was the issue. The only way we could leave was to pay for a seat with the press convoys that were allowed to travel out of Iraq by protected convoys into Jordan.

Our lovely Iraqi neighbours said they would let us know when it was safe to make the 20 km trip into the centre of Baghdad to organise a trip out. One of our neighbours offered to take us in his van. It was decided that we would all leave together, so a date was set. We had to leave at 7am. However, at the last minute, David refused to join as he thought it was unsafe and he didn't want to lose his film footage. This delayed everyone as we did not want to leave without him. An hour later, he agreed to go. We were horrified to see the carnage, dead bodies on roads, buses of civilians bombed with all the occupants still inside burnt alive. It was gruesome beyond belief, but we had to take David's photos out as evidence of war.

We finally arrived at Firdos Square to find that the press convoy had already left. There was one press car left. The driver agreed to take us but said it was high risk as we were easy targets for local Iraqi bandits and there was no guarantee that we could get across the border into Jordan. We said: 'We will take the risk,' which we did. Three times, when the driver saw a bandit roadblock ahead, he made a huge detour either to the left or right for some kilometres to successfully bypass the bandit.

It was a great relief to arrive at the Jordanian border. When we had come into Iraq on the same road, we had been processed first on the Jordanian side leaving Jordan, and then again on the Iraqi side to check our bona fides and all equipment. While these checks were undertaken, we had tea and a chance to chat with the Iraqi border guards. To our surprise, when the return convoy arrived at the same place, the Iraqi border compounds were all bombed flat, and instead, there were two huge US trucks blocking the highway. We showed our British, US and Australian passports and were waved through with lots of messages and camaraderie from the US border soldiers who were bored being there alone most of the rest of the day.

Back in Jordan, Ruth stayed again at the friendly hotel which the owner had put at the human shield's disposal. There we met other human shields who had come there in earlier convoys. There was a great celebration and relief to be away from the war zone, but grief also, to think about the hardships ahead for the local Iraqi civilians.

Ruth Russell in Iraq

Ruth's Return to Adelaide after being a Human Shield

Ruth returned home to Adelaide. To her surprise, she was often stopped on the street by strangers who said, 'thanks for going to Iraq to oppose this war'. It seemed the war and her involvement were well publicised. She was again invited to tell her story on Channel Seven TV and has given many talks on her experiences.

Her first public talk was with Natasha Stott Despoja who had supported her throughout. Interestingly, the Editor of *The Advertiser* was in the audience, and later that morning he phoned her to say how moving her story was, but he was not prepared to publish it! What a double standard – she was disgusted with his response. It didn't matter though as Ruth continued to give many talks over the following months, around Adelaide, Australia and in New Zealand. People did want to know what really happened and thanked her for speaking for them.

Ruth says that the lesson from all this is clear:

Never be afraid to speak out for what is right, no matter what – build strategic allies and a support base. You can't fool Australians really that this war was ever 'just'. It was a risk but really, all life is a risk – I could be killed in a car accident tomorrow, so what seems a risk can often be mitigated with backup support. Your own conscience will tell you what is the right thing to do.

Let us hope a situation like this never happens again. If it does, Ruth expects thousands to join the human shield movement as people *can* make a difference. Better ways exist to resolve conflict through the UN Security Council so all weapons could be destroyed so that peaceful resolution of conflicts become mandatory.

In 2003, WILPF Australia organised a national project - *Children of the Gulf War*. This was an international photographic exhibition on the effects of depleted uranium on Iraqi children. Chris Henderson (WILPF Qld) organised for it to be shown in all capital cities of Australia.

You are invited to the Adelaide launch of the

Children of the Gulf War
photographic exhibition
by

Ruth Russell, "human shield" in Baghdad, March - April 2003

at The Barr Smith Library, University of Adelaide
on Tuesday 10 June 2003 at 5.30 p.m.

Please RSVP by 6 June 2003:
Phone: 8278 2150
Email: bandmarnott@hotmail.com

WILPF Australia national project: 'Children of the Gulf War'
photographic exhibition on the effects of depleted uranium on Iraqi
children, Adelaide, 2003

Ruth Russell 'Human Shield in Iraq. Finding a Way Forward for Peace', Seaview Press, Adelaide, 2005

Ruth Russell, 2003
State Library SA

[1] 'United Nations Security Council and the Iraq War' En.m.Wikipedia.org.

[2] 'United Nations Security Council and the Iraq War' En.m.Wikipedia.org.

[3] 'United Nations Security Council and the Iraq War -History' En.m.Wikipedia.org.

7

United Nations Security Council Resolution 1325 on 'Women, Peace and Security'

Background

This resolution was adopted unanimously on 31 October 2000 to acknowledge the disproportionate and unique impact of armed conflict on women and girls. WILPF worked collaboratively with other key international women's organisations to promote the best ways forward for women to achieve peace, security and freedom, wherever they live.

There were prior ground-breaking, influential developments. At the *UN Fourth World Conference on Women*, held in Beijing, China, on 4-15 September 1995 to honour the 50th anniversary of the founding on the United Nations, it was recognised that although the status of women has advanced in some important respects, progress had been uneven, inequalities between women and men have persisted, and major obstacles remain, with serious consequences for the well-being of all people.[1]

WILPF are proud that it was an Australian WILPF woman, Felicity Hill, then Director of our WILPF UN Office in New York, who took the lead in this new international initiative by working with the UN Member States' representatives to draft and get through the United Nations Security Council the first resolution about the impact of war on women, UNSCR 1325 on *Women, Peace and Security*. The resolution stresses the importance of women's full and equal participation in conflict resolution, peacebuilding, peacekeeping and in post-conflict reconstruction. This is a positive step forward to protect women and girls and give them a voice and place on all decision-making issues relating to women, peace and security.

In SA, Women *in Black* monthly vigils were held on Parliament House steps for eight years. SA branch women's campaign to *Keep Space for Peace* continued for ten years, raising awareness of the danger of proliferating space and making a contested area likely to become a war zone which could have disastrous consequences for everyone on earth.

Women in Black vigils, Parliament House, Adelaide

In Australia, WILPF women were already meeting regularly in Canberra with other key national women's organisations, so this was the place to gather both national and local support from all women's groups in Australia. The Australian Government in Canberra, through their National Office for Women, set up regular meetings through the YWCA so that two representatives from each national women's organisation could attend. It was an exhilarating experience to meet with over one hundred representatives from women's sporting, academic, multicultural, youth and specific groups like our WILPF peace organisation to discuss women's peace and security issues.

When news of this historic UN Security Council resolution became known among our Australian women's groups, there was much enthusiasm to proceed. WILPF Australian Section subsequently received a government grant to establish a specific UNSCR 1325 website, which they did in 2004. This project was now on our Australian women's national agenda. The next step was to consider what women wanted to work on to achieve the goals of this project.

Then Prime Minister, John Howard, did not like these large, collaborative national women's gatherings, so he decided to split us into four different groups, hoping to weaken our collective activism. Our last big meeting with every national women's group attending was to be held at Broken Hill, where WILPF was to lead the debate on how to proceed with UNSCR 1325. Our WILPF National Coordinator spoke to this new international initiative that would benefit all women and gained full support from the representatives of all the national women's organisations.

Soon after this meeting, women's groups had to decide which of the four smaller categories we would join. WILPF chose to join the human rights group auspiced by the YWCA. We were saddened by the breakup of the larger group which gave good support to smaller organisations and migrant women's issues.

As WILPF at the international level had taken a key role on this new UNSCR 1325 initiative, WILPF at our Australian national level, was invited by the Federal Office for Women, to research and put forward a clear action plan on how to implement UNSCR 1325 in Australia. This entailed receiving a grant from the Office for Women to pay for more research on what was needed, as well as to then take our ideas to women's groups in all capital cities, to consult widely with them, and bring back the best possible implementation program.

WILPF had the background research done by Di Zetlin, assisted by Rachel Litster, from Queensland University, and was able to engage Professor Elisabeth Porter from the University of South Australia to run the consultations in May and June 2009 in Adelaide, Brisbane, Canberra, Sydney, Darwin, Perth, Melbourne and Hobart. It was a huge task, accomplished well, despite a tight time frame. The 189 participants attending the consultations represented 88 different organisations.

Key national consultation findings include:[2]

- There is overwhelming support for UNSCR 1325.
- There is extremely strong agreement on the need to develop an Australian National Action Plan (NAP) on UNSCR 1325, with differences of view on how this might practically occur.
- We can learn from the 14 plans already written, of the need to include: diversity; a national and international focus; broad understandings of peace and security; and a clear matrix.
- There was widespread agreement of the need for a strong champion of 1325. Most participants believed that while the Minister for the Status of Women should be centrally involved, the leadership of the implementation also requires the portfolios of Prime Minister and Cabinet, and Ministers for Foreign Affairs, Defence, Trade, Immigration and Citizenship, Families, Housing, Community Services and Indigenous Affairs and the Attorney-General. Some pacifists, believing there should be no army or weaponry, find it problematic to be in negotiation with the Department of Defence on issues of peace.
- There is a strong consensus that a NAP should have both a national and international focus.
- Most participants agreed that there are clear connections between the prevention of conflict, the protection of women and girls during conflict, women's participation at all levels of

decision-making and the need for prosecution of gender-based war crimes. Some felt that increasing participation of women (in peacekeeping, peacemaking, peacebuilding and political decision-making) should be prioritised.
- The development of a NAP should be premised on broad definitions of peace and security.
- There is vast agreement that human rights, development, education and women's empowerment are critical components of the process of furthering peace and security for women and girls and must be explicitly addressed.
- There is strong support for a NAP to be built around an action plan matrix with measurable targets, Ministerial and agency responsibilities defined clearly, budgets, timelines, accountability and evaluation.
- The need for an inclusive, consultative process to develop a NAP was stressed repeatedly. Many participants urged the need to listen to the voices of refugees who have recently come from war-torn zones as well as listening to indigenous women, diverse inter-faith groups, women's NGO and academics.
- There is great evidence of the need for Peace Studies to be taught in schools and in universities

The first *Australian National Action Plan 2012-2018* was launched on International Women's Day, 8 March 2012.

Australian National
Action Plan, 2012-2018

A collective of key women representatives then formed an advisory *Australian Women Peace and Security Coalition*, to work with the Australian Government as it implemented this first plan and prepared for a second national action plan. WILPF had Barbara O'Dwyer and Ludmilla Kwito both from out WILPF ACT Branch, ably representing us on this national committee.

Col Amanda Fielding (ADF) and Barb O'Dwyer (WILPF), Annual Civil Society Dialogue, Canberra, 2015

The second edition is called the *Australian National Action Plan on Women, Peace and Security, 2021-2031*.[3]

Australian National
Action Plan on
Women, Peace and
Security, 2021-2031

The principles of the second National Action Plan include:

- a 'do no harm' approach;
- gender mainstreaming;
- a human rights-based approach; and
- recognising and responding to diverse experiences.

The Plan aims to:

- support women and girls' meaningful participation and needs in peace processes;
- reduce sexual and gender-based violence;
- support resilience, crisis and security, law and justice efforts to meet the needs and rights of all women and girls; and
- demonstrate leadership and accountability for Women, Peace and Security.

WILPF integrates these principles and aims in an ongoing evaluation of the outcomes of the Plan.

Moving from the International to the National and Local

In 2015, the South Australian Government was planning an international Defence meeting and invited key European NATO members to their conference at the Adelaide Convention Centre. Three days before the conference was to start, Barbara O'Dwyer and Ruth Russell (WILPF's then Joint National Coordinators), were asked could we attend, with apologies for the late invitation.

When the conference opened, both Barbara and Ruth were there representing WILPF. We were pleased to find the NATO Chairperson begin the conference proceedings by first publicly acknowledging WILPF's great international work in getting UNSCR1325 operational. The Chairperson told the local representatives that they always included the local

WILPF women in their national security conferences. The look of sheer amazement on the faces of the local politicians was conspicuous. They treated us 'as equals,' something they were not used to doing.

WILPF Australia has built good relations since with the *Australian Civil-Military Centre*, based in Canberra, which has taken on the role of implementing this UNSCR 1325 project.

Sadly though, WILPF SA branch has not been invited to any more SA Government defence conferences since. Maybe we should take the initiative and ask to be invited again.

We are pleased that this project is now in its second three-year program.

[1] 'Beijing Declaration from the Fourth World Conference on Women', Beijing, China 4-15 September 1955.

[2] Elisabeth Porter (with Ruth Russell) 'The Final Report: Developing a National Action Plan on United Nations Security Council Resolution 1325,' (WILPF Australian Section, 2009).

[3] https://www.dfat.gov.au/sites/default/files/australias-national-action-plan-on-women-peace-and-security-2021-2031.pdf

8

SA WILPF, 2005-2014

WILPF SA Activities

WILPF women continue to actively work to promote peace.

WILPF SA Branch, 2005

In 2005, on WILPF's ninetieth birthday, a weeklong *Women's Festival of Peace* was held in the Legislative Assembly Exhibition Space, in Canberra.

WILPF SA Branch, 2006

In 2006, the SA Branch hosted the WILPF Triennial Conference in Adelaide, *Women's Wellbeing, Peace and Care: Challenges for Government Economic Policy.*

WILPF SA Branch, 2007

In 2007, Ruth Russell and Sue Gilbey from SA attend WILPF's 19th Triennial International Congress in Santa Cruz, Bolivia.

WILPF Congress
Programme, 2007

Sue Gilbey at the
conference

WILPF SA Branch, 2008

In 2008, WILPF instigated the call for a 'Women, Peace and Security' Australian National Action Plan, as outlined in the previous chapter. WILPF set up a *Civil Society Network* of academics and NGOs to work together on overseeing this implementation.

WILPF SA Branch, 2009

In 2009, WILPF QLD hosted the WILPF Australian Section Triennial Conference and set out WILPF's programme of work:

- Challenging Militarism;
- Investing in Peace; and

- Strengthening the United Nations.

WILPF SA Branch, 2011

Our SA Branch had been busy ever since we set up in this state in the 1960s, so it was decided to hold a celebratory exhibition for a month in the large conference room at the Box Factory community centre. It was amazing to see how many different topics we had dedicated our energies to over the last fifty years. Labor governments were in power, both in Canberra and South Australia and supportive of women's rights. There was a sense of optimism that a better future was possible for everyone.

Planning this exhibition was an enjoyable experience as we found so much interesting material that covered our many campaigns over the last 75 years. We completely transformed the large empty room with all our colourful posters, tea towels and information about the important campaigns we had participated in for so many years.

Our exhibition was launched by Vanessa Swan, Director of the SA Office for Women on Friday 29th April 2011, to a full house. We received congratulatory comments from everyone, and History SA photographed the posters and gave us a copy for our records. We thanked Dr Bev Hall who donated two large peace paintings to hang in the entrance hall, then later, in the United Nations' office in Carrington Street.

On 12 April 2011, SA WILPF raised awareness of the *Global Day of Action against Military Spending*. Over the last ten years, SA WILPF women have held some event every year to highlight the increasing amount of money spent on weapons and their destructive capabilities. WILPF members, Maureen Arnott, Leonnie Blumson, Ruth Russell and Tina Namow blew whistles and handed out flyers to shoppers in Rundle Mall, flyers about the huge amount of money being spent on weapons instead of providing for civilians needs.

The State Labor Government promoted itself on car number plates as 'The Defence State'. It began encouraging local weapons manufacturers to support local state high schools by providing laptops and other equipment with the payback that they would be officially named a 'Defence School' and the brightest pupils would be encouraged to join the weapon manufacturers' companies, and there are plenty of them in this state.

WILPF women campaigned against this iniquitous partnership with schools, but as it was a time of slight downturn in the local economy, many parents said they 'were just happy if their child had a job'. Dr Bev Hall took the lead on this campaign in the Northern suburbs and over several years was able to influence some School Principals and parents *not* to be involved in this scheme.

On 28 June 2011, the SA Defence Industry Expo was held at the Adelaide Convention Centre. WILPF worked with other groups who had formed *Left Unity*, an activist group of organisations and individuals to plan a full day of action which attracted much attention and positive responses.

On 2 September 2011, the *International Day of Peace* was celebrated. WILPF was pleased to partner again with the *Medical Association for the Prevention of War* (MAPW), the *Australian Peace Committee*, the *United Nations Association*, the *Graham F Smith Peace Trust*, *Quakers*, *Psychologists for Peace* and the *City of West Torrens* to hold an inspiring day at Emmanuel College. Many students' art and sculptures for peace filled halls and classrooms. Crowds of visitors and students listened to students' talk about their work through poetry, music and drama throughout the day. It was an inspiring day and bode well for peace in the future.

Another excellent peace program was being run at the time to accredit junior primary, high schools and even kindergartens as *UN Peace Schools*. The accreditation program was run by *Save the Children* for many years.

In November, WILPF members held a successful quiz night for both WILPF and the *Support Association for the Women of Afghanistan* (SAWA), providing a good boost to our funds.

WILPF SA Branch, 2012

In January, the rally *Take a Stand Against Racism* was held on the SA

Parliament House steps in solidarity with the Aboriginal Campaign and the launch of the book *This is what we said: Australian Aboriginal people give their view on the Northern Territory Intervention*. WILPF supported this rally and provided funds for several Aboriginal speakers to travel from NT to speak at the rally.

WILPF women enjoyed the International Women's Day march which started at the UniSA West Campus then marched to Parliament House for some rousing speeches and carried on to the laws in front of the State Library where awards were given to honour several women's work. WILPF's longest serving member, Cynthia James, received the *Barbara Pilkington Award* for her many years of service to peace.

WILPF women from all the Australian branches met up at our *WILPF Triennial Conference* in May 2012 at Kings Cross, Sydney NSW. It was opened by Penny Williams, *Australia's Global Ambassador for Women*. We worked together to develop our Australian Programme of Work for the next three years. At the end of the conference, we felt connected and ready for whatever future campaigns needed to be rolled out.

An *Independent and Peaceful Australia Network* (IPAN) was formed. Key Australian national peace groups decided to work together through this new network to promote an independent Australian foreign policy and oppose foreign military bases in Australia. WILPF SA is part of our local IPAN group which feeds into this national network. Over 50 Australian groups have joined, making this an effective network for peace.

WILPF International ran a global campaign opposing the coming UN Arms Trade.

International Human Rights Day was celebrated on 10 December 2012.

WILPF member, Sue Gilbey, worked with other organisations to hold a book launch of *A Decision to Discriminate: Aboriginal Disempowerment in the Northern Territory*. This event was well attended.

Throughout the year WILPF women attended many other events on climate change, human rights, women's prison reform and other WILPF related issues in another busy year.

WILPF SA Branch, 2013

WILPF women held our meetings in the UNAA office in Carrington Street. We continued participating in our local weekly radio program which was now in its sixth year.

In January, Maureen Arnott and Ruth Russell organised a display in the Stirling Library and gave a public talk showing a film about the United Nations Security Council Resolution 1325 *Women, Peace and Security*.

In March, on the tenth anniversary of the war in Iraq, Ruth Russell gave a talk on her experience there as a *human shield* during that catastrophic war which has since destabilised that whole area.

For *UN International Day of Peace* on 21 September 2013), WILPF hosted speakers from all the local peace and social justice groups to update everyone on their current campaigns.

For November, WILPF women participated in the *Global Peace School* event organised by *Save the Children*, showcasing peacebuilding activities through dance, music, video recordings and presentations by school students and teachers. It was great to witness the student's enthusiasm.

WILPF members attended the *SafeGround* (previously Australian Network to Ban Landmines) AGM, led by Catholic Sister Patricia Pak Poy, which included the documentary *If you love this planet* by Dr Helen Caldicott. A young university student, Catriona Stanfield, representing the *International Campaign to Abolish Nuclear Weapons* (ICAN) Australia also spoke of the momentum building to ban nuclear weapons.

WILPF supported our local support group for Afghan women - *Support Association for the Women of Afghanistan* (SAWA) to publish a book *Two Trees* with women artists from Australia and Afghanistan displaying their artwork. We enjoyed the book launch and book.

Dr Bev Hall was nominated by WILPF and entered onto the *SA Women's Roll of Honour* for her work with Indigenous peoples and peace work over more than thirty years.

Tina Namow and Dr Amanda Ruler are part of a new Port Adelaide local action group, raising concern about uranium (yellowcake) being trucked to our port, loaded on ships and returned to WA for disposal.

WILPF women celebrated the end of our year with a party and group photo taken with a sign *Say No to Violence* which will be put on our WILPF international website as part of their campaign. It had been another busy year!

In 2013, there was a call to rise in defiance of injustices women suffer with mass action to end violence against women. The SA Branch continue to work on this *Say No to Violence Against Women* campaign.

WILPF women say NO TO VIOLENCE AGAINST WOMEN, 2013

Coralie Nicholls,
WILPF International
'One Billion Rising
Against Violence,' 2013

In 2013, the WILPF SA branch was involved in the *Muckaty Photographic Exhibition* launch where Aboriginal land at Muckaty, Northern Territory was chosen for a nuclear waste dump by the Australian Government. In June 2014, halfway through Federal Court proceedings launched by Traditional Owners, the Federal Government agreed to not further pursue the site.

Traditional Owners released the following statements after hearing their campaign had been successful. Marlene Nungarrayi Bennett, Warlmanpa woman said,

> Today will go down in the history books of Indigenous Australia on par with the Wave Hill Walk-off, Mabo and Blue Mud Bay. The Warlmanpa Nation has won an eight-year battle against the might and power of the Commonwealth Government and Northern Land Council. Justice has prevailed and this is a win for all Territorians.

MUCKATY Exhibition photo of Muckaty traditional land and people

WILPF SA Branch, 2014

The highlight for our year was a big celebration with all the local peace groups and churches for *International Day of Peace* on 21 September 2014.

WILPF organised a huge *Community Peace Festival* with twenty local social justice groups attending this event in Scots Church on North Terrace. The welcoming address was delivered by the Moderator of the Uniting Church in Australia, Synod of South Australia, Dr Deidre Palmer, and former Senator Rosemary Crowley was in fine form as MC. Professor Lis Porter from the University of South Australia gave a positive, thought-provoking talk on *Building Peace*.

Stephen Darley from IPAN followed up with a more sobering presentation on militarisation in the Asia Pacific. Teachers from Parafield Gardens *Global Peace School* and *Kindergarten* spoke about their peace program with kindergarten children.

A recorded peace message from Yoko Ono and John Lennon singing his immortal *Imagine*.... was played, courtesy of the United Nations

Association. Then it was time to meet and greet other peace friends and learn about their current campaigns. At the end of the day, we felt better connected, refreshed and ready to continue to speak out for peaceful resolutions of all issues.

A WILPF social event and discussion night was held on 30 October. The topic was *Our understanding on the war in the Middle East*. Discussion included the early history of Iraq and the complexities of great powers making decisions that affect the lives of the diverse communities that make up Iraq today. Sustainable peace cannot be achieved without their full participation. We want to hear their voices including those of women from that region.

On *International Human Rights Day* on 10 December, WILPF partnered with UNAA's presentation of *The United Nations Human Rights Day Public Lecture by* Emeritus Professor Ivan Shearer, AM, RFD, FAAL. Prof Shearer spoke on the topic *International Protection of Human Rights by UN Bodies: Is it Effective?* drawing mainly on his experience of eight years as a member of The United Nations Human Rights Committee, working in Geneva and New York.

Several WILPF women went to long-term member Molly Brannigan's 90th birthday on 16 November. She was presented with a special framed message of thanks for her long service to WILPF and the wider women's movement.

WILPF SA women Ruth Russell and Sue Gilbey have been regular broadcasters for eight years on Radio Adelaide *A Peace of the Action* program every Sunday 11.30-12 noon.

Ruth interviewing an Afghan woman who came to Australia as an asylum-seeker and is now attending University.

In April 2014, the *Global Day of Action against Military Spending* saw SA women actively promoting awareness on the amount of money spent globally on military weapons.

Leonnie Blumson,
Rundle Mall, 2014

Ruth Russell, Tina Namow, Leonnie Blumson and Maureen Arnott
hand out 800 flyers, Rundle Mall, 2014

Tina Namow, WILPF member, is involved in the Port Adelaide campaign to raise awareness of issues around yellowcake being transported from WA to be shipped from Port Adelaide.

Port Adelaide campaign against transport of yellowcake

Vale - Heather Southcott - President of the SA United Nations Association, Former Leader of the Australian Democrats, Member of Parliament and long-time WILPF member. Heather was a committed WILPF member, the first woman to lead a Parliamentary political party in Australia. She invited WILPF to be on the United Nations SA Committee and the UN Status of Women committee. WILPF was instrumental in getting a plaque acknowledging Heather's great contribution to peace and women's rights added to the memorial plaques honouring outstanding SA citizens on the North Terrace pavement.

9

WILPF Centenary Celebrations, 2015

WILPF Celebrations

With the WILPF Australian Patron's support, then Governor-General of Australia, Quentin Bryce AD, CVO, WILPF held a national exhibition and conference in Canberra. Each WILPF branch organised their own centenary celebrations. In 2015, WILPF had five active branches in Queensland, New South Wales, ACT, Tasmania and South Australia. We celebrated our centenary at the international, national and local levels.

WILPF International Centenary

As outlined in earlier chapters, at a meeting at The Hague, in April 1915, women from across the world, from nations at war as well as those still neutral such as the United States, resolved to form an *International Committee of Women for Permanent Peace*, which became the *Women's International League for Peace and Freedom*.

As mentioned in an earlier chapter, two already existing Australian organisations formed in Melbourne in 1915, the *Sisterhood of International Peace* and the *Women's Peace Army*, affiliated with the international organisation. The motto of the Sisterhood of International Peace was *Justice, Friendship and Arbitration*. Central to these women's anti-war mobilisations was an idea that had purchase in Australia – that conflict should be resolved through negotiation, arbitration and conciliation.

In April 2015, *WILPF International Centenary Conference* took place in The Peace Palace, The Hague, the Netherlands. Thirteen women from Australia and New Zealand organised their own 'peace train' from Istanbul to The Hague.

One hundred years ago, more than 1,100 women from twelve countries travelled across Europe to the Netherlands to debate ways to end the first world war and prevent further conflict. The story has already been told of how three Australian women joined them: Eleanor Moore, Vida Goldstein and Cecilia Johns. Eleanor Moore returned to Melbourne and established a women's peace group which affiliated with Women's International League for Peace and Freedom when they formally adopted that name in 1919.

In 2015, ten Australian women and three women from New Zealand WILPF, met in Istanbul, Turkey, and took their own peace train to The Hague to join the WILPF centenary celebrations. South Australian women Leonnie Blumson and Ruth Russell travelled on the re-enacted peace train with others from the Queensland branch.

Along the way they were given an extravagant reception in Budapest, Hungary, in honour of the achievements of the early WILPF women; were interviewed for local television and radio programs; and arrived to join their WILPF sisters at the Peace Palace in the beautiful grounds of the International Court of Justice, at The Hague, Netherlands.

When they arrived, they met with more Australian WILPF women who had flown in, including Frances Bedford MP, Stephanie Key MP and Dr Bev Hall with her family from Adelaide who joined our SA group. Frances came dressed up as South Australian suffragette *Muriel Matters* who had attended the 1915 Congress, then devoted her life to helping the British suffragettes achieve the vote for women.

Amber Rudd, Home Secretary of the UK and Frances Bedford, 2016
The Muriel Matters Society, UK

It was an emotional and stirring event being led by our dynamic leader, Madeleine Rees. It was pleasing to see more women from Africa joining WILPF so that we could say that our organisation now truly represents women from every corner of the world. There were many stirring speeches and events to invigorate and inspire all to dedicate afresh to promoting peace in the future. As older members fade away, our organisation continues to attract more younger women who are taking up the challenge to promote peace and freedom for all.

It was a privilege to be in the company of five Nobel Peace laureates, including Leymah Gbowee, who was involved in the mass mobilisation of women in Liberia to demand an end to civil war, and also Jody Williams who launched the international campaign to successfully ban land mines.

Edith Ballantyne, Secretary-General of WILPF international for 23 years and its International President for six years, was especially honoured. She mentioned in her address that 'as a teenager she had fled Nazi occupation of Czechoslovakia'. In her speech, she reflected that '100 years later, we have not stopped war, and in fact we face many wars, so this is both a great and a sad day.'

Two WILPF Presidents have received the Nobel Peace prize. Jane

Addams who became our first President, was awarded the prize in 1931, followed in 1945 by Emily Balch, who attended the 1915 Congress and led the organisation from 1935.

Jane Addams

Emily Balch

UN Security Council Resolution 1325, unanimously adopted in 2000, has yet to bring the change campaigners want. Women still do not have a seat at the peace negotiating table. 'When it comes to the crucial moment, the door is closed,' said Madeleine Rees when WILPF's Secretary-General. Madeleine told us that our Hague conference will feed into a UN review of women's role in peace and security to tie in with the 15th anniversary of the resolution. Radhika Coomaraswamy, the lead author of the UN review, also spoke later at this conference.

The three plenaries explored the power dynamics in society and how they can be challenged, the increase in global militarisation and the structural root causes of war, and what activists can do to bring change at local, national and international levels.

For Madeleine Rees, engaging activists is one of her main aims of the conference. She said:

> We've got to stop disengaging, stop engaging in football or consumerism or anything that makes us avoid paying attention to what is happening...It starts with an individual decision – I will participate in making a difference to commit to think global and act local; we need that. We are not going to make demands of governments or the United Nations so much, instead we are looking at the work we need to do ourselves. The thing is for us - going back to local engagement.

Rees suggested that 'local engagement could involve challenging local politicians on their stance on nuclear weapons, or campaigning against the arms trade, violence against women or trafficking'. She questioned the use of killer robots which are piloted remotely.

Cynthia Enloe, a Professor of Political Science at Clark University in Massachusetts USA, and a specialist in demilitarisation, adds that local people need to watch for signs that trouble is brewing. She said:

> Men are often encouraged to be the nation's protectors ... and maintain their role as household protectors, and that role of protector really can be manipulated by people wanting to encourage the annexation of neighbouring territories or to build up the military. One thing to look out for is governments or warmongers, who try to encourage men to merge these two roles.

Edith Ballantyne hopes the anniversary conference will result in a 'powerful call' to work together to achieve an end to militarisation, ultimately realising the vision of Jane Addams and the women who travelled to the Hague in 1915.'[1]

The Hague, 2015

'Women Stop War' Conference in Canberra, May 2015

Madeleine Rees, then WILPF International Secretary-General, attended our *Women Stop War Conference* in Canberra. Natasha Stott Despoja AM, Australian Government *Ambassador for Women and Girls*, 2013-2016, welcomed a women's delegation from Afghanistan, and of course, Madeleine Rees. She opened our conference by acknowledging WILPF Australian women's long involvement in WILPF, 'demonstrating right from the get-go, that very particular Antipodean insistence on challenging the status quo, on bringing women's voices to the fore.'

Natasha quoted our WILPF foremother Jane Addams,

> What after all has maintained the human race on this globe despite all the calamities of nature and all the tragic failings of mankind, if not faith in new possibilities and courage to advocate for them....certainly that courage was characteristic of the Sisterhood of Peace and has run through the veins of Australian peace advocates.

In welcoming Madeleine Rees, Natasha referred to the landmark year of 2015, a time to celebrate WILPF and milestones that advance the rights of women, including *UN Security Council Resolution 1325* and other resolutions that have followed, all with 'WILPF's fingerprints all over them.' She noted the 20th anniversary of the *Beijing Declaration and Platform for Action*, the *UN Millennium Development Goals* and 70 years of the United Nations.[2]

WILPF National Centenary Exhibition, Canberra

Back in Australia we had a big conference in Canberra attended by our international WILPF leader, Madeleine Rees, who inspired all with her passion and leadership to create a better world. It was an inspiring and beautiful experience to be part of. Our first woman Australian Governor, Dame Quentin Bryce AD CVO, opened a huge, impressive WILPF exhibition in Canberra, we were given a special postal commemoration stamp and revered Professor Marilyn Lake gave a stirring speech applauding our huge contribution to peace over one hundred years.

A prestigious *National Centenary Exhibition* was organised by long time Canberra WILPF member, Margaret Bearlin and held in Canberra, the political capital – showcasing one hundred years of women's activism. The local *Chorus of Women* choir sang songs composed especially honouring WILPF women's activism over one hundred years.

Historical Exhibition, Canberra Museum and Art Gallery, 2015
Photo by Janette McLeod

Renowned feminist historian Professor Marilyn Lake AO, FAHA, FASSA opened the national exhibition by acknowledging the Indigenous elders past and present of the country on which we meet. She said:

Let us celebrate the contribution of, among others, Eleanor Moore, Vida Goldstein, Edith Waterworth, Mabel Drummond, Doris Blackburn, Anna Vroland, Nancy Wilkinson, Margaret Holmes, Oodgeroo Noonuccal, Mildred Thynne, Margaret Thorp, Margaret Forte, Maud McBriar, Lorraine Mosely, Jean Richards, Fran Boyd, Shirley Abraham, Irene Greenwood, Evelyn Rothfield, Freda Brown, Betty King, Stella Cornelius, Nancy Shelley, Kay Mundine, Cathy Picone, Lyn Lane, Ruth Russell, Chris Henderson, Helen Cooke, Eve Masterman, Barbara O'Dwyer. There are of course many, many, others whom we should recognise across all states and territories.

Marilyn acknowledged that individual names and the collective effort for peace and freedom both matters. She looked forward to the day when there is recognition of the 'distinctive contribution made by women to the achievement of freedom and democracy in our country and across the world'.

To contextualise this, given the commemoration of the centenary of the Gallipoli landing, she reminded participants that 'so many others of us seek recognition of the fact that the outbreak of war generated a vigorous anti-war movement in Australia and elsewhere.' For example, 'the commemoration of WILPF's long history of peace activism reminds us of an international movement initiated by the women of the world, in which Australians played an important role from the beginning.'

Lake contrasted so-called 'manly individual Anzac virtues such as endurance, resourcefulness, candour, independence, comradeship, patriotism, chivalry and loyalty' with WILPF's emphasis on honouring 'the universal and collective values of freedom, peace, human rights and social justice.'

In 1915, Vida Goldstein declared her opposition to war 'because it is based on fear and hate and lies'. Wars generate fear and hatred and lies that provoke more violence. WILPF challenges the dominant official histories circulated in Australian schools with the wisdom and insight of women's history.

Lake reminded members that in Australia, WILPF's affiliated groups, the Sisterhood of International Peace and the Women's Peace Army were among those organisations whose efforts contributed to the defeat of conscription in 1916 and 1917 and the gathering pressure to secure a negotiated peace settlement, which became ALP policy by mid-1918. She recognised that WILPF members were bitterly disappointed with the conditions of armistice and the subsequent Treaty of Versailles, whose punitive, vengeful, terms against Germany they condemned as 'revenge sowing the seeds of another world war'.

Linking back to the direction of this chapter, Professor Lake acknowledged the timely and important exhibition in Canberra which documents WILPF's activism in support of peace education and disarmament in the 1920s and 1930s, in securing 117,000 Australian signatures for a world-wide disarmament petition, the highest per capita number of signatures collected anywhere. It suggests a determinedly anti-war Australian sentiment prevailed in Australia.

She reminded the audience that in the decades following World War 2, WILPF advocates such as Doris Blackburn and Anna Vroland in Victoria 'worked to ban or limit nuclear weapons and to oppose the establishment of the Woomera Rocket Range on Aboriginal land.' As mentioned in earlier chapters, WILPF became involved in campaigns for Aboriginal land, citizenship rights and justice in the 1950s and 1960s.

From the 1960s, WILPF members opposed the misguided Vietnam war and conscription and the establishment of US bases on Australian soil. They drew attention to rape in war and violence done to women and children. They also campaigned for the inauguration of peace studies in schools and universities and the building of a peace memorial in the national capital.

Lake reminded us that WILPF remains a *woman-based, woman-focussed organisation*, invoking the common interests and solidarity of women across the world. An exciting new development, documented in the exhibition, is the formation of *Young WILPF* in Australia by women including Sharna da Lacy and Cara Gleeson, who attended the meeting of the *Commission for the Status of Women* in New York in 2014.

Lake called attention to ongoing wars across the Middle East, in the Ukraine and in parts of Africa and to the millions of refugees fleeing Syria and other conflict zones. Her cry was that: 'It surely behoves Australia to adopt a more generous and proactive refugee and asylum seeker policy in this time of need.' This is pertinent considering Australia's treatment of asylum seekers, especially the incarceration of children, many who are locked up for lengthy periods. This practice of detention is an international disgrace and a source of national shame. Lake encouraged WILFP to 'extend their efforts now to demand the freedom of these *Forgotten Children*, the victims of Australian injustice.'

Exhibitions like this WILPF one point to the significance of documenting the past to provide information and inspiration for present and future understanding. As Kate Laing has noted in her La Trobe University Ph.D. thesis on the history of WILPF, when Queensland member Margaret Thorp attended the Vienna meeting of WILPF in 1921, she spoke in support of presenting appropriate history in school texts so that the human progressive movement be given prominence.

The WILPF centenary exhibition provided the sort of materials that detail the women who helped to make history, women who have over generations worked to achieve democracy and freedom for Australians, equal rights for women and men, and now additionally demand recognition of the equal humanity of asylum-seekers, refugees and their children. The ideals of peace and freedom have inspired WILPF in Australia and internationally for one hundred years and continue to do so.

SA WILPF Branch Centenary celebrations

WILPF SA branch held our own WILPF Centenary elaborate exhibition of our one-hundred-year history in the Hawke Centre, University of South Australia. It was a marvellous event. We had made huge displays of one hundred years of our history and displayed them around the hall. There were speeches by our longest serving WILPF SA Branch member, Cynthia James, who gave a stirring speech giving tribute to all the WILPF women in South Australia who have actively engaged with all the peace issues of our time. WILPF National Coordinator Barbara O'Dwyer from Canberra and others also gave speeches.

Long-time WILPF member Cynthia James' opening address at our
WILPF centenary exhibition, 2015

Eric Bogle came to sing his famous song *And the band played Waltzing Matilda* and John Schuman's anti-Vietnam war song, *I was only nineteen*. The Allegria Choir sang the 1915 song *I didn't raise my son to be a soldier*. The hall was packed with well-wishers and completely bedecked in every space possible with symbols and memorabilia from one hundred years of women's peace activism. It was a wonderful celebration.

Eric Bogle singing, 2015

The Hon Stephanie Key, Labor Member for Ashford, gave a speech in SA Parliament on Tuesday 16 June 2015 acknowledging WILPF in celebrating its 100th anniversary. She recalled that in 1915 at the first conference, Muriel Matters was the only South Australian in attendance, smiling at how Frances Bedford Independent Labor Minister came dressed as Muriel at the celebrations, one hundred years later. She paid tribute to WILPF's long-term work for peace. She cited the way that Jane Addams, WILPF's first international President, was received by then US President Woodrow Wilson after the congress. He hailed the ideas she brought from the conference and adopted nine as part of the 14 points for the World War I peace negotiations. As mentioned, Addams received a Nobel Prize for her work in peace.

Key also recognised Emily Greene Balch, a WILPF activist and international Secretary, the second WILPF member to receive a Nobel Peace Prize in 1946. She noted how blessed she was in having Leymah Gbowee from Liberia present at the international conference in 2015.

Gbowee was awarded a Nobel Prize in 2011 for 'non-violent struggle for the safety of women and for women's rights to full participation in peace-building work'. Key also mentioned Shirin Ebadi from Iran who, in 1997, was awarded a Nobel Peace Prize for her efforts for democracy and human rights, focusing especially on the struggle for the rights of women and children, was also a speaker.

Key recognised that the organisation, Women's International League for Peace and Freedom, was awarded a peace prize because of the work it had done over the years. She said:

> In South Australia we have a very active Women's International League for Peace and Freedom, and I remember very clearly that they were involved in a number of campaigns to try to get people to think about what peace means and how we can achieve it.[3]

WILPF women continue to work for universal peace and freedom – however long that takes to achieve! We realise that working for a more peaceful world can be an enjoyable and artistic experience working with other likeminded people who want our children and grandchildren to inherit a less violent world, one that values peace and honours human endeavour. Hopefully, the next generation will join us as we continue to promote peace and freedom for all.

We are pleased you have followed our actions over the last one hundred years and invite you to come and join us as there are plenty of issues still to be addressed before we can say we are living in a peaceful world. It is a worthwhile and enjoyable use of your time to work towards creating a more peaceful world. We look forward to meeting you soon.

WILPF SA members Leonnie Blumson, Bev Hall, Ruth Russell, Irene Gale, Maureen Arnott with WILPF President Chris Henderson, 2019

WILPF International 2022-2025

In 2022, WILPF International has 41 Sections and Groups across Africa, the Americas, South Asia, Asia Pacific, Europe and the MENA region. Many of these operate in areas of conflict. In summary, it is pertinent to note that *WILPF SA* continues to support *WILPF International*. Since the 2018-2021 International Programme, there are significant global challenges, including growing climate and environmental crises, a global pandemic, the erosion of democracies, and the devastating impacts of militarisation. In articulating the *International Programme for 2022-2025*, WILPF reiterates its vision:

> A world of permanent peace built on feminist foundations of freedom, justice, nonviolence, human rights, and equality for all, where people, the planet, and all its other inhabitants coexist and flourish in harmony.[4]

The *values* of WILPF International include:

- Equality and human rights
- Anti-militarism
- Nonviolence
- Solidarity
- Anti-racism
- Ecological sustainability
- Care and community
- Integrity.

The *approach* to this international programme is a commitment to a *feminist approach to peace* built on:

- Collaboration and participation
- Strength in diversity
- Persistence
- Intersectionality
- Learning and sharing
- Transforming power
- Centring lived experience.

WILPF is committed to evolving with the rapidly changing context of the world. This includes the interrelated systems of oppression that permit and perpetuate inequalities of militarism, nationalism, capitalism, racism and colonialism. All these power struggles are rooted in patriarchal concepts of power and supremacy and continue to keep sustainable peace and freedom out of reach for most of the world's population.

WILPF SA branch are clear:

> We will continue working towards our collective vision of feminist, permanent peace built on foundations of freedom, justice, nonviolence, human rights, and equality for all.

WILPF members collaborate on their common goal:

We are united in our determination to study and make known the root causes of war, and we work to abolish the legitimisation, practices, tools, and mindsets of war. We believe thinking and acting transformatively can create a future in which permanent peace is possible.[5]

WILPF Australia Triennial Conference, 2021

[1] www.theguardian.com/global-development/2015/apr/27/female-activists-hague-new-peace-agenda-1915-congress-of-women.

2 ww.dfat.gov.au. speeches Women's International League for Peace & Freedom (WILPF)
WomenStopWar centenary conference.

[3] Speech by Hon Stephanie Key, in SA Parliament on Tuesday, 16 June 2015 (as recorded in Hansard).

[4] WILPF International Programme 2022-2025. Wilpf.org

[5] Ibid.

Ruth Russell B.Ed, Dip T, is on the South Australian Women's Honour Roll. Ruth is proud to have this opportunity to share with you our SA WILPF history.

Ruth's childhood was spent with her missionary parents at the remote Kunmunya Aboriginal mission in the Kimberleys where her progressive parents worked to support three diminishing Aboriginal tribes to foster independence, pride in their skills and loving care to their homeland. This experience taught Ruth that all people are worthy of full citizenship, agency and to live fulfilling, productive lives, while maintaining their culture and history.

Ruth was lucky enough to travel the world and work in New Zealand and England before returning to Australia to settle in Adelaide in the 1970s, marry and have two children. She met up with WILPF women in the 1990s and decided to join this dynamic, caring and progressive group who also wanted to ensure that everyone has an equal and valued right to live in peace. Sadly, there is a lot more to be done before this ideal becomes a reality.

By sharing our stories, Ruth hopes to inspire more people to stand up for truth, justice and equality so that everyone can experience peace and freedom.

www.ingramcontent.com/pod-product-compliance
Lightning Source LLC
Chambersburg PA
CBHW072005290426
44109CB00018B/2142